LONGMAN
KEYSTONE

C

Workbook

Anna Uhl Chamot

John De Mado

Sharroky Hollie

PEARSON
Longman

LONGMAN
KEYSTONE C

Keystone C Workbook

Copyright © by Pearson Education, Inc.

Pearson Education, 10 Bank Street, White Plains, NY 10606

Staff credits: The people who made up the *Longman Keystone* team, representing editorial, production, design, manufacturing, and marketing, are John Ade, Rhea Banker, Liz Barker, Danielle Belfiore, Don Bensey, Virginia Bernard, Kenna Bourke, Anne Boynton-Trigg, Johnnie Farmer, Maryann Finocchi, Patrice Fraccio, Geraldine Geniusas, Charles Green, Henry Hild, David L. Jones, Lucille M. Kennedy, Ed Lamprich, Emily Lippincott, Tara Maceyak, Maria Pia Marrella, Linda Moser, Laurie Neaman, Sherri Pemberton, Liza Pleva, Joan Poole, Edie Pullman, Monica Rodriguez, Tania Saiz-Sousa, Chris Siley, Lynn Sobotta, Heather St. Clair, Jennifer Stem, Siobhan Sullivan, Jane Townsend, Heather Vomero, Marian Wassner, Lauren Weidenman, Matthew Williams, and Adina Zoltan.

Smithsonian American Art Museum contributors: Project director and writer: Elizabeth K. Eder, Ph.D.; Writer: Mary Collins; Image research assistants: Laurel Fehrenbach, Katherine G. Stilwill, and Sally Otis; Rights and reproductions: Richard H. Sorensen and Leslie G. Green; Building photograph by Tim Hursley.

Cover Image: Background, John Foxx/Getty Images; Inset, Alex Bloch/Getty Images
Text composition: TSI Graphics
Text font: 11 pt ITC Stone Sans Std
Photos: 4, James Randklev/ChromoSohm Media Inc./Photo Researchers, Inc.;
14, David Young-Wolff/PhotoEdit; 21, Steve Cole/Photodisc/Getty Images;
28, Steve Shott/Dorling Kindersley; 39, Digital Stock/CORBIS; 46, Catherine Huerta;
53, Andreas Schlegel/Alamy; 60, J. Helgason/Shutterstock; 71, Shutterstock;
78, Photos.com; 85, Craig Orback; 92, Tom and Pat Leeson/DRK Photo;
103, Raymond Forbes/age fotostock america; 110, Catherine Huerta; 117, Shutterpoint;
124, James Young/Dorling Kindersley; 135, Ian O'Leary/Dorling Kindersley;
142, Cornelius Van Wright; 149, Photos.com; 156, Hulton Archive Photos/Getty Images;
167, Shutterstock; 171, NASA/Johnson Space Center; 174, Julian Baum/Dorling Kindersley;
181, Shutterstock; 188, Bettmann/CORBIS.
Illustrations: Catherine Huerta, 46; Craig Orback, 85; Catherine Huerta, 110;
Rosanne Kaloustian, 142
Technical art: TSI Graphics

ISBN-13: 978-0-13-233980-3
ISBN-10: 0-13-233980-3

PEARSON LONGMAN ON THE **WEB**

Pearsonlongman.com offers online resources for teachers and students. Access our Companion Websites, our online catalog, and our local offices around the world.

Visit us at **pearsonlongman.com**.

Printed in the United States of America
2 3 4 5 6 7 8 9 10 11–CRS–12 11 10 09 08

Contents

Unit 1

Unit 2

READING 1

READING 2

READING 3

READING 4

Unit 3

READING 1

READING 2

READING 3

READING 4

Unit 4

READING 1

READING 2

READING 3

READING 4

Unit 5

READING 1

READING 2

READING 3

READING 4

Unit 6

READING 1

READING 2

READING 3

READING 4

UNIT 1 How can change improve people's lives?

READING 1: "The First Americans"

VOCABULARY **Key Words** *Use with textbook page 5.*

Write each word in the box next to its definition.

climate	customs	irrigate	natural resources	nomads	tribe

Example: ___*climate*___ : the typical weather conditions in an area

1. _____: a group of people of the same race, beliefs, and customs

2. _____: all the land, minerals, and energy in a country

3. _____: acts or practices that people in a society do because of tradition

4. _____: to supply water to land or crops

5. _____: people who move from place to place, usually to find land for their animals

Use the words in the box at the top of the page to complete the sentences.

6. The villagers were glad to meet the people from a nearby _____ and learn some of their customs.

7. When people live on dry land they _____ their crops and fields.

8. They lived as _____ and moved every few years to find new land for their animals to graze.

9. She introduced him to the _____ and practices of the tribe.

10. The _____ in southern California is just about perfect.

Read the paragraph below. Pay attention to the underlined academic words.

The Sonoran Desert spreads out over 100,000 square miles. It is located in the southwestern <u>region</u> of North America. Except for the rainforests of South America and Africa, the Sonoran Desert is home to more plants and animals than any other area of its size. The hot dry <u>environment</u> of the desert <u>affects</u> the way the plants and animals live. They have learned to survive with the little water <u>available</u> to them. The kangaroo rat, for example, gets water from seeds.

Write the letter of the correct definition next to each word.

Example: __*b*__ environment   **a.** produces a change in someone or something

_____ **1.** available   **b.** the land, water, and air in which people, animals, and plants live

_____ **2.** region   **c.** able to be used or seen

_____ **3.** affects   **d.** large area

Use the academic words from the exercise above to complete the sentences.

4. Pollution does great harm to the _____, changing the quality of the land, water, and the air.

5. The Great Plains are a flat, grassy _____ of the United States.

6. Your behavior always _____ your friends and family.

7. The book is not _____ at the library yet.

Complete the sentences with your own ideas.

Example: The teachers are available ___*to help their students*___.

8. I like to study in a(n) _____ environment.

9. _____ always changes how people dress.

10. I live in a region that _____.

WORD STUDY **Spelling Long *a* and *e*** *Use with textbook page 7.*

> **REMEMBER** The long vowel sounds /a/ and /e/ can be spelled several different ways. Long *a* can be spelled *a* as in *labor*, *a_e* as in *make*, *ai* as in *maid*, *ay* as in *day*, and *ea* as in *break*. Long *e* can be spelled *e* as in *he*, *ee* as in *bee*, *ea* as in *pea*, *eo* as in *people*, and *y* as in *lady*.

Read the words in the box below. Then write each word in the correct column in the chart.

clang	evil	create	capacity	leader
afraid	mustang	meow	equal	greater
hay	reader	guarantee	shape	raise
grape	leo	Monday	electricity	agree

/a/ spelled a	/a/ spelled a_e	/a/ spelled ai	/a/ spelled ay	/a/ spelled ea
clang				

/e/ spelled e	/e/ spelled ee	/e/ spelled ea	/e/ spelled eo	/e/ spelled y

Write the letter-sound pattern in each word below.

Example: main *long /a/ spelled ai*

1. scream _____

2. escape _____

3. straight _____

4. Thursday _____

5. sea _____

6. spree _____

REMEMBER Preview the text before reading it by looking at the title, headings, and any visuals. Read the first and last sentences of each paragraph. Ask yourself about the topic to see what you know already. Previewing helps you set a purpose for reading.

Look at the article below and answer the questions that follow.

Mountainous Region of the Western United States of America

Mountain Ranges

The Western United States of America is home to several mountain ranges. They span Colorado to California and Montana to New Mexico. People travel to the mountains to climb, camp and ski. Some visitors go just for the beautiful views and the clear mountain air.

The Sierra Nevada, Cascade and Coastal Ranges spread across the west coast of the United States and into Mexico and Canada.

The Rocky, Sierra Nevada, Cascade and Coastal Ranges

The Rocky Mountain Range spans over 2000 miles from Mexico to Alaska. It is made up of over 100 smaller mountain ranges. The highest peak in the range is near Leadville, Colorado.

1. Read the title and headings. What do you think the article is going to be about?

   _____

2. What does the picture tell you about the topic of the article?

   _____

3. Read the first and last sentences in each paragraph. What more did you learn about the article?

   _____

4. What do you already know about the topic?

   _____

5. How can previewing help you understand an article?

   _____

COMPREHENSION   *Use with textbook page 14.*

Choose the best answer for each item. Circle the letter of the correct answer.

1. One theory is that the first Americans came from _____.

   a. Europe   **b.** Asia   **c.** Australia

2. Once they began using horses, the Plains people lived as _____.

   a. nomads   **b.** farmers   **c.** hermits

3. The tribes of the southeast were forced to move west by _____.

   a. the seasons   **b.** disease   **c.** European settlers

4. Native customs were strongly affected by _____.

   a. climate   **b.** travel   **c.** language

5. The Native Americans of the Southwest learned to _____.

   a. grow crops with   **b.** catch snakes   **c.** build wooden homes
   very little water

EXTENSION   *Use with textbook page 15.*

Research five Native American tribes. Find out where they lived and tell what state or states are in that area now. Try to find tribes that lived near where you live now.

Tribe	Homeland Area Today
Navajo	New Mexico, Utah, Arizona

Order of Adjectives *Use with textbook page 16.*

REMEMBER Adjectives give information about people, places, or things. When more than one adjective describes the same noun, the adjectives must be listed in this order: (1) opinion or quality, (2) size, (3) age or temperature, (4) shape, (5) color, and (6) material.
Example: Her beautiful long red hair is always in her face.

Complete the charts below with adjectives from the box.

tall	good	excellent	clay	blue	stone	freezing	rectangular	enormous	old

Opinion or Quality	Size	Age or Temperature

Shape	Color	Material

Write sentences using the adjectives in parentheses in the correct order before the noun given.

Example: (brick / red / cozy) house *Some day I want a cozy red brick house.*

11. (rocky / cold / small) place

_____

12. (green / unusual / plastic / square) wastebasket

_____

13. (leather / black / brand-new / cool) jacket

_____

14. (old / tall / confident) woman

_____

15. (brown / young / friendly) dog

_____

WRITING A DESCRIPTIVE PARAGRAPH

Describe a Group of People *Use with textbook page 17.*

This is the T-chart that Katie completed before writing her paragraph.

Group
Cherokee

Trait	Example
good builders	*constructed houses of river cane and plaster* *built larger seven-sided buildings for ceremonies*
created wonderful artwork	*made beautiful baskets out of river cane* *carved wooden masks for ceremonies and battles*

Complete your own T-chart about another Native American tribe or group of people.

Group	
Trait	**Example**

How can change improve people's lives?

READING 2: From *Riding Freedom*

VOCABULARY **Literary Words** *Use with textbook page 19.*

REMEMBER A **plot** is the sequence of related events in a story. Most plots contain one or more conflicts. A **conflict** is a struggle between opposing forces. It moves the story forward and makes it more interesting.

Write *yes* if each situation describes a conflict. Write *no* if it does not.

Conflict?	Situation
yes	Aliyah wants dessert but her mother tells her to study instead.
1.	The two dogs snarled at one another.
2.	Raúl picked up the tennis ball and threw it to Maria.
3.	The wind howled. I didn't want to go back into the storm.

Write one or two sentences in each row illustrating a conflict between the following person or thing.

People/Things	Sentences
two people who want the same object	*Edgar and Astrid crossed their arms. They both yelled at the same time, "That's mine!"*
4. person versus mountain	
5. doing the right thing versus doing the easy thing	

VOCABULARY **Academic Words** *Use with textbook page 20.*

Read the paragraph below. Pay attention to the underlined academic words.

> During the 1960s in the United States, more and more women wanted to work outside the home. However, many faced <u>discrimination</u>. They had trouble finding work. If they did find work, they were often paid less than men. Women fought for equality by holding marches and speaking out for their rights. Over time, this helped change people's <u>attitudes</u> about women in the work force. Women finally <u>achieved</u> equality in the workplace. Today, to deny a person a job based on gender is <u>illegal</u>.

Write the academic words from the paragraph above next to their correct definitions.

Example: *discrimination*: unfair treatment of some people because of their race, ethnic group, religion, or gender

1. _____: succeeded in doing something, especially by working hard

2. _____: not allowed by law

3. _____: thoughts or feelings about something or someone

Use the academic words from the paragraph above to complete the sentences.

4. It is _____ to drive without a driver's license.

5. Different people have different _____ about politics.

6. She worked hard all her life and _____ great things.

7. Most people want to eliminate _____ in the workplace.

Complete the sentences with your own ideas.

Example: In the past, _____*my ancestors*_____ suffered from discrimination.

8. My attitude toward _____ has changed over time.

9. _____ achieved wonderful things in life.

10. I know that it is illegal to _____.

REMEMBER When an ending is added to a single syllable word that ends in a vowel + a consonant, the final consonant is doubled, as in *spin/spinning*. If the word has more than one syllable, the consonant is doubled if the stress is on the final syllable, as in *control/controlling*.

Add an ending as directed to each word. Write the word in the last column.

Base Word	+ Ending	= New Word
hop	-ed	*hopped*
1. sit	-ing	
2. submit	-ed	
3. pat	-ed	
4. orbit	-ing	
5. shop	-ing	

Create a new word by adding the ending *-ed* or *-ing* to each word below.

Example: begin + _ing_ = _____beginning_____

6. fasten + _____ = _____

7. spot + _____ = _____

8. omit + _____ = _____

9. slip + _____ = _____

10. clap + _____ = _____

READING STRATEGY | ANALYZE HISTORICAL CONTEXT

Use with textbook page 21.

REMEMBER Analyzing historical context can make a text more meaningful and easier to understand. Pay attention to events, location, and characters' reactions. Think about what you already know about the events or setting.

Read the paragraph and answer the questions that follow.

The Day After

Yesterday, on September 11th, when the towers fell, everything was chaos. When I arrived at the soup kitchen the next morning, I was surprised by how organized the workers were.

"Are you here to help?" asked a man behind the table.

"Uh…Yeah, I am."

"Good. They need some help down at that end of the table," he said.

I started to help a woman who was putting sandwiches on plates and handing them out. Firefighters and police started to file by. Some were covered in dust. All of them looked tired. Some would eat and leave, but others would stay and talk.

At the end of the day, the man in charge of the soup kitchen came by.

He said, "Thanks for the help today. Can you come back tomorrow?"

"You bet," I said. I couldn't imagine staying in my apartment uptown. I needed to be here. I needed to help.

1. When does the story take place?

   _____

2. Where does the story take place?

   _____

3. What historical event had just happened in the place and time of the story?

   _____

4. What is the main character's reaction to the events that have taken place around her?

   _____

5. How can knowing the historical context of a story help you to understand its meaning?

   _____

Choose the best answer for each item. Circle the letter of the correct answer.

1. Charlotte pretended to be "Charley" to _____.

    a. make friends   **b.** run for office   **c.** run her business

2. Since she was a woman, Charlotte had to register to vote _____.

    a. disguised as a man   **b.** in a dress   **c.** with a male friend

3. Everyone asked Charley _____.

    a. who she would vote for   **b.** why she was dressed like a man   **c.** why she registered to vote

4. The men in town thought that women should _____.

    a. vote like their husbands   **b.** stay out of politics   **c.** fight for their rights

5. The real Charlotte Parkhurst's identity was discovered _____.

    a. by a traveler who worked with her   **b.** when she tried to vote   **c.** after she died

RESPONSE TO LITERATURE *Use with textbook page 29.*

Write a short paragraph describing how you think Charlotte might have felt on her ride to town. Was she scared? Excited? Ready for a fight? Did she think of her friend Hayward?

_____

_____

_____

_____

_____

GRAMMAR, USAGE, AND MECHANICS

Sequence Words *Use with textbook page 30.*

> **REMEMBER** Sequence words describe the order in which events take place. Common sequence words are *first, then, next,* and *finally. First* and *finally* introduce the first and last things that happened. *Next* and *then* can be used to introduce anything that happened in between. Most of these sequence words need a comma after them, but *then* does not need a comma.
> **Example:** First, we went to dinner. Then we went to the movies. Next, we got ice cream, and finally, we walked home through the park.

The sentences below present events in the order in which they happened. Add the sequence words from the box to help readers understand the order of events. Be sure to use a comma when needed.

Finally	Next	Second	First	Then

1. _____ he came home from school.

2. _____ he took his books from his knapsack.

3. _____ he did his homework.

4. _____ he checked his homework.

5. _____ he put his books back in his knapsack and watched some television.

The sentences below present a series of events in the wrong order. Write *First, Second, Then, Next,* or *Finally* to show the correct order.

6. _____ we found seats in the movie theater.

7. _____ we stood in line to buy tickets.

8. _____ we watched the movie.

9. _____ we went to the movie theater.

10. _____ we bought our tickets.

WRITING A DESCRIPTIVE PARAGRAPH

Describe an Event or Experience *Use with textbook page 31.*

This is the sequence-of-events organizer that Haley completed before writing her paragraph.

First
I had my hair done at a professional salon.

↓

Next
I put on makeup and small amounts of glitter.

↓

Then
I put on my black dress and high heels.

↓

Finally
My escort arrived to pick me up.

Complete your own sequence-of-events organizer about an exciting event you participated in or attended.

First

↓

Next

↓

Then

↓

Finally

Name _____ Date _____

UNIT 1

How can change improve people's lives?

READING 3: "Early Inventions"

VOCABULARY **Key Words** *Use with textbook page 33.*

Write each word in the box next to its definition.

| designer | device | elements | invention | patent | periodic table |

Example: _____*device*_____ : a machine or other small object that does a special job

1. _____: someone who thinks of ideas for creating something and then draws patterns so they can be made

2. _____: something new that is made for the first time

3. _____: simple chemical substances made of one type of atom

4. _____: a specially arranged list of simple chemical substances

5. _____: a document that says you have the right to make or sell an invention

Use the words in the box at the top of the page to complete the sentences.

6. The class is studying all the known chemical _____.

7. She built a _____ out of some old machine parts in her basement.

8. The engineer applied for a _____ to protect his new

_____.

9. We made a model from the sketch drawn by the _____.

10. We need to look up a chemical symbol. Do you have a science textbook that shows

the _____?

Read the paragraph below. Pay attention to the underlined academic words.

> In March 2007, a boat <u>created</u> by a Swiss company made history by sailing across the Atlantic Ocean. The boat had solar panels on its roof whose <u>function</u> was to collect sunlight. This <u>technology</u> allowed the boat to cross the Atlantic using only solar energy. The journey proved that the sun can be a <u>significant</u> source of energy.

Write the letter of the correct definition next to each word.

Example: ___*b*___ function   **a.** made or invented

_____ **1.** significant   **b.** the purpose of something

_____ **2.** technology   **c.** noticeable or important

_____ **3.** created   **d.** all the knowledge and equipment used in science

Use the academic words from the exercise above to complete the sentences.

4. The machine is very complicated, but its _____ is not clear.

5. New _____ allows people to travel and communicate in new ways.

6. The invention of the printing press was a _____ event.

7. The painter _____ a beautiful new work of art for the gallery.

Complete the sentences with your own ideas.

Example: I think that new technology has made ___*communication much easier*___.

8. One important function of a fence around a yard is to

_____.

9. Once my friends and I created a(n) _____.

10. I spend a significant amount of time on _____.

WORD STUDY **Nouns That Modify Nouns** *Use with textbook page 35.*

> **REMEMBER** A noun names a person, place, thing, or idea. Sometimes a noun can function as an adjective to modify (describe) another noun. For example, *piano* is a noun because it names an object. In the phrase *piano music*, *piano* is an adjective because if modifies the noun *music*. Knowing that a noun can modify a noun helps you use words correctly.

Read each sentence. Then circle the noun modifier and underline the noun being modified.

Example: They ate their (evening) meal.

1. We have a new grocery store in the neighborhood.

2. They sell good breakfast cereal.

3. I like fruit drinks because they are healthful.

4. The package design really gets your attention.

5. You can learn a lot from television advertisements.

Add a noun to modify each noun to complete each sentence.

Example: Charles makes _____*potato*_____ soup

6. Matt got a _____ puppy.

7. Lucille uses too much _____ spray.

8. The _____ towel has a beautiful pattern.

9. Rico buys a _____ ring.

10. The dog likes to chew _____ toys.

Use with textbook page 35.

> **REMEMBER** Recognizing sequence helps you understand the order in which things happen. Look for words that show sequence, such as *first, then, next, finally, last, while, during,* and *after.* Look for dates and times.

Read the paragraph and answer the questions that follow.

> ## Bessie Coleman
>
> On June 15, 1921, Bessie Coleman became the first African-American woman to earn a pilot's license. She got her license in France. Then she returned to the United States and participated in flight shows. In the 1920s, flight shows were one of the few ways that pilots could make a living flying. During this time, Bessie became a figure in the media because she was a woman and an African-American who had a pilot's license. She also performed daring stunts.
>
> Although she liked her work and her new-found fame, the next thing she wanted to do was open a flight school for African Americans. Sadly, Bessie died in a plane accident before realizing her dream. But her bravery has inspired many people to pursue their dreams no matter what the obstacles. Today, all Americans can finally pursue their dreams.

1. What is the first event that happens in the passage?

   _____

2. What is the next event that happens in the passage?

   _____

3. What did Coleman do while she was a pilot?

   _____

4. What is the final event described by the passage?

   _____

5. How can understanding the order of events help you when reading a story?

   _____

Name _____ Date _____

Choose the best answer for each item. Circle the letter of the correct answer.

1. Nineteenth-century inventions sped up travel and _____.

   a. traffic   **b.** mathematical calculation   **c.** communication

2. Levi's jeans are named after the man who _____.

   a. provided money to   **b.** made jeans with rivets   **c.** led the California
   gold miners   Gold Rush

3. The first vacuum cleaners were _____.

   a. too big to fit inside   **b.** too small for home use   **c.** so valuable they
   the home   were often stolen

4. The first bubble gum was invented by an _____.

   a. child   **b.** soldier   **c.** accountant

5. "Cat's eyes" make it safer to _____.

   a. fly at night   **b.** swim at night   **c.** drive at night

EXTENSION   *Use with textbook page 41.*

Choose five objects that you use today. Research each object to find when and where it was invented. Fill in the chart below.

Object	Origin
pencil	England, 1600s

GRAMMAR, USAGE, AND MECHANICS

Simple Past: Regular and Irregular Verbs *Use with textbook page 42.*

> **REMEMBER** The simple past describes events or actions that began and ended in the past. Form the simple past of regular verbs by adding *-d* or *-ed* to the base form. If a verb ends in a consonant, sometimes you must double it before adding *-ed*. If a verb ends in a consonant and *y*, change the *y* to *i* and add *-ed*. If a verb ends in a vowel and *y*, just add *-ed*. The past form of many common verbs is irregular. Those forms must be memorized.

Complete each sentence below with the correct form of the verb in parentheses.

1. (know) She _____ the answer.

2. (be) There _____ problems with the first transatlantic cable.

3. (transform) Inventions _____ society.

4. (put) He _____ his jeans in the washing machine.

5. (dry) My grandmother always _____ her laundry on a clothesline.

Answer each question below using the simple past. Use the same verb that is used in the question.

Example: What did he need at the mall?

   He needed a pair of jeans. _____

6. What did you think of the story?

   _____

7. What did the artist create?

   _____

8. How many people did the storm affect?

   _____

9. Where did he find that old typewriter?

   _____

10. How did he reply to the invitation?

   _____

20   Unit 1   •   Reading 3

WRITING A DESCRIPTIVE PARAGRAPH

Describe an Object *Use with textbook page 43.*

This is the word web that Pablo completed before writing his paragraph.

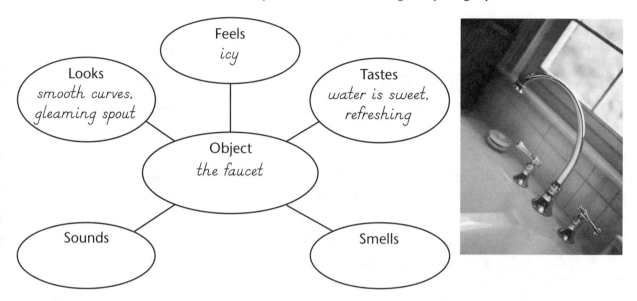

Complete your own word web for a paragraph about an object that you have used, eaten, or worn.

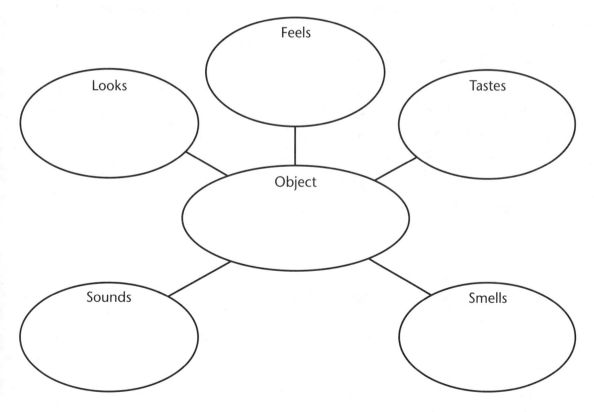

READING 4: From *Seedfolks*

VOCABULARY **Literary Words** *Use with textbook page 45.*

> **REMEMBER** **Imagery** is descriptive language used in literary works. Imagery is created by using sensory details. **Setting** is the time and place of the action of a story. Sensory details help establish the setting in the reader's mind.

Each sentence establishes its setting or action with sensory details. Label each sentence with the sense it refers to: smell, taste, touch, sight, or sound.

Sense	Description
touch	The hot sand was rough against her feet.
1.	Night had turned the whole town dark gray and black.
2.	The fruit drink was too sugary sweet for me.
3.	The evening breeze brought the faint scent of the autumn leaves through the window.

Read the passage below. Then answer the questions.

> The broad leaves high above us were deep green with hints of yellow and red. Thin beams of light touched the soft ground. Colorful tropical birds called out in strange voices. The dirt below us was moist, and small drops of water fell to the ground. Our guide told us to look up, and we saw two monkeys swinging from a branch. They chattered back and forth like people. The air was warm and sweet.

4. What is the setting of the passage? _____

5. List the sensory details that help establish the setting.

_____

_____

VOCABULARY Academic Words *Use with textbook page 46.*

Read the paragraph below. Pay attention to the underlined academic words.

> One day my teacher asked our class to come up with a plan to help make our school a more beautiful place. With this <u>goal</u> in mind, I noticed that an old garden bed <u>located</u> next to the parking lot was filled with weeds. In class the next day, I suggested that the class plant a garden there. My teacher and classmates <u>reacted</u> with excitement to my idea. The whole class got <u>involved</u> in planning and planting the new garden.

Write the academic words from the paragraph above next to their correct definition.

Example: _____*located*_____: in a particular place or position

1. _____: included in a project or situation

2. _____: behaved in a particular way because of what someone has said or done

3. _____: something you want to do in the future

Use the academic words from the paragraph above to complete the sentences.

4. Our community garden is _____ on Gonzalez Avenue.

5. Everyone _____ with shock when the news came.

6. She worked all summer to reach her _____.

7. The whole team was _____ in the project.

Complete the sentences with your own ideas.

Example: We learned that many statues are located in _____*Italy*_____.

8. I reacted to the good news by _____.

9. My family likes to get involved in _____.

10. I have a goal this year to _____.

REMEMBER An apostrophe (') is used to show possession with a noun. Add *'s* to the end of a singular noun, such as *book of the girl* → *girl's book*. Add just the apostrophe to the end of a plural noun, such as *books of the girls* → *girls' books*. An apostrophe is also used to take the place of missing letters in a contraction. For example, *it* and *is* become the contraction *it's*.

Look at the chart below. Form the possessive of each phrase. Write the possessive in the chart.

Phrase	Possessive Form
the ideas of the boy	*the boy's ideas*
1. the suggestion of Dr. Greene	
2. the toys of the child	
3. the strength of the waves	
4. the laughter of Mona	
5. the petals of the flowers	

Look at the chart below. Form the contraction for each pair of words. Write the contraction in the chart.

Word 1	Word 2	Contraction
I	am	*I'm*
6. you	are	
7. is	not	
8. who	is	
9. they	are	
10. he	will	

READING STRATEGY | **VISUALIZE** *Use with textbook page 47.*

REMEMBER When you visualize, you make pictures in your mind of what you are reading.

Read the paragraph and answer the questions that follow.

I was standing at the edge of the stage, behind the curtain, waiting for my turn in the dance recital. It was an Irish Step dance and I was wearing my step shoes, black tights and a green shirt. Last year, I performed in the recital with a group. But this year, it was just me. My palms felt sweaty. I heard my name announced, and I walked out on stage. There I was, on the stage, by myself. The lights were so bright I couldn't see the audience. For a moment, it felt like no one was there. I kept that thought in my head as I danced. It made it seem as if I were performing for a row of lights, not 200 people. My routine seemed effortless. When I finished I heard applause.

1. What is the passage about?

_____

2. What is the strongest image in the passage?

_____

3. How do the images help you to make a mental picture of the scene?

_____

4. Draw a picture of the scene described in the passage. Be sure to include details from the passage in your drawing.

```



```

5. How can the skill of visualizing help you to understand a text more clearly?

_____

Choose the best answer for each item. Circle the letter of the correct answer.

1. Kim wants to make her father's spirit proud because _____.

   a. he often praised her   **b.** he never knew her   **c.** he was angry with her

2. Kim used the vacant lot to plant _____.

   a. beans   **b.** flowers   **c.** carrots

3. Wendell helps Kim by _____.

   a. giving her advice   **b.** buying her   **c.** watering the plants
   about when to   more beans
   plant beans

4. Next, Wendell will most likely _____.

   a. plant his own garden   **b.** move out of the area   **c.** talk to Kim about
                                                                  her plants

5. In this story, the neighbors _____.

   a. are afraid of each other **b.** don't like each other **c.** look out for each other

RESPONSE TO LITERATURE   *Use with textbook page 55.*

Imagine that you live in the building with Ana, Kim, and Wendell. One day you look out your window and see someone planting flowers in the vacant lot. What do you feel when you see them? What will you do next? Will you join them in the garden? Write a short paragraph to describe the situation.

_____

_____

_____

_____

_____

GRAMMAR, USAGE, AND MECHANICS

Comparative and Superlative Forms of Adjectives *Use with textbook page 56.*

> **REMEMBER** A comparative adjective + *than* compares two things. *The* + a superlative adjective compares three or more things. For most one-syllable adjectives, form the comparative by adding *-er* and the superlative by adding *-est*. One-syllable adjectives (consonant-vowel-consonant): double the last consonant and add -er/-est.
> **Examples:** This math test is *harder* than last week's. That tomato is the *biggest* one in the market.
> For most two-syllable adjectives ending in *-y*, change the *y* to *i* and add *-er* or *-est*.
> **Example:** The *scariest* Halloween was two years ago at my aunt's haunted house.
> Add *more* or *most* before most other adjectives of two or more syllables.
> **Example:** The public pool is *more exciting* than the library.
> Some adjectives have irregular forms.
> **Example:** This is the *worst* dress I have tried on today.

Complete each sentence with the correct form of the adjective in parentheses.

Example: (bright) The stars today are _____*brighter than*_____ they were yesterday.

1. (icy) The sidewalk is _____ than the driveway.

2. (serious) He is the _____ student in the class.

3. (good) Broccoli tastes _____ than spinach.

Write sentences with comparative and superlative adjectives. Follow the directions in parentheses.

Example: (Use the superlative form of *large*.)

  *That is the largest house in the neighborhood.*_____

4. (Use the comparative form of *intelligent*.)

_____

5. (Use the superlative form of *thin*.)

_____

WRITING A DESCRIPTIVE PARAGRAPH

Describe a Place *Use with textbook page 57.*

This is the three-column chart that Nicole completed before writing her paragraph.

The Garden		
Back	**Middle**	**Front**
corn stalks	*tomatoes, eggplants*	*squash, carrots*

Complete your own three-column chart for a paragraph describing a place you are familiar with.

Back	**Middle**	**Front**

Name _____ Date _____

Read the paragraph below carefully. Look for mistakes in spelling, punctuation, and grammar. Mark the mistakes with proofreader's marks (textbook page 460). Then rewrite the paragraph correctly on the lines below.

Everyone in the family was excited for our trip. my sister was home from school. I had not seen her in more than six months. on the day before we left, we had to pack our bags I packed my toothbrush a summer hat and five pairs of socks. I put them into my large backpack, Then I choosed two warm shirts and one light one. I also packed a smallest brown bag just for the car ride. it was a gift from my grandmother. I put two books in the bag so i could read them on the way to the cabin My parents told me to bring a bottle for water, too. I wanted to bring my dog Buster, but he had to stay home. Dogs are not allowed to stay on the cabin with families. But even without buster, we had a wonderful time.

_____

_____

_____

_____

_____

_____

_____

_____

Underline the vocabulary items you know and can use well. Review and practice any you haven't underlined. Underline them when you know them well.

Literary Words	Key Words	Academic Words	
plot	climate	affects	created
conflict	customs	available	function
imagery	irrigate	environment	significant
setting	natural resources	region	technology
	nomads	achieved	goal
	tribe	attitudes	involved
	designer	discrimination	located
	device	illegal	reacted
	elements		
	invention		
	patent		
	periodic table		

Put a check by the skills you can perform well. Review and practice any you haven't checked off. Check them off when you can perform them well.

Skills	I can . . .
Word Study	☐ spell and pronounce long *a* and *e*. ☐ recognize and spell double consonants. ☐ recognize and use nouns modifying nouns. ☐ use apostrophes.
Reading Strategies	☐ preview. ☐ analyze historical context. ☐ recognize sequence. ☐ visualize.
Grammar, Usage, and Mechanics	☐ use correct adjective order. ☐ use sequence words. ☐ use regular and irregular simple past verbs. ☐ use comparative and superlative forms of adjectives.
Writing	☐ describe a group of people. ☐ describe an event or experience. ☐ describe an object. ☐ describe a place. ☐ write a descriptive essay.

Name _____ Date _____

Learn about Art with the Smithsonian
American Art Museum *Use with textbook pages 66–67*

LEARNING TO LOOK

Look at *Storm King on the Hudson* by Samuel Colman on page 67 in your textbook.
Place a blank sheet of paper over the right half of the painting. Write down three
details that you see on the left side of the painting. State facts, not opinions.

Left Side

Example: *There is smoke from the steamship.* _____

1. _____

   _____

2. _____

   _____

3. _____

   _____

Now move the blank sheet of paper over to cover the left half of the painting.
Write down three details that you see on the right side of the painting. State facts,
not opinions.

Right Side

4. _____

   _____

5. _____

   _____

6. _____

   _____

INTERPRETATION

Look at *Storm King on the Hudson* again. Imagine a day in the life of the men in the fishing boat on the right side of the painting. What would their day be like? Write your answers below.

Men in Fishing Boat

Example: _It is very hot out here._

_____

_____

_____

Now imagine a day in the life of the men on the steamship on the left side of the painting. What would their day be like? Write your answers below.

Men in Steamship

_____

_____

_____

5W&H

Look at *Fermented Soil* by Hans Hofmann on page 66 in your textbook. Write six questions you would like to ask the artist about this painting.

Example: _What color did you use first?_

1. Who _____

2. Where _____

3. When _____

4. What _____

5. Why _____

6. How _____

Name _____ Date _____

What are the benefits of facing challenges?

READING 1: "The Train to Freedom" / "Follow the Drinking Gourd"

VOCABULARY **Key Words** *Use with textbook page 71.*

Write each word in the box next to its definition.

| fugitive | heritage | network | runaway | shelter | Underground Railroad |

Example: ___*runaway*___: someone who has left home or the place where he/she is supposed to be

1. _____: group of people or organizations that are connected or that work together

2. _____: a network of people who helped slaves escape to freedom during the 1800s

3. _____: someone trying to avoid being caught, especially by the police

4. _____: the traditional beliefs, values, and customs of a family, group, or country

5. _____: protection from weather or danger

Use the words in the box at the top of the page to complete the sentences.

6. The police searched everywhere for the _____ who had escaped from jail.

7. We looked for _____ when it started to rain.

8. My friend learned that in 1856, members of his family escaped slavery through the

_____.

9. The _____ enslaved man sneaked out of the slave master's home in the early hours of the morning.

10. When Amy lost her dog, Max, a _____ of friends helped her find him.

Read the paragraph below. Pay attention to the underlined academic words.

During World War II, the United States military wanted to create a <u>code</u> that could not be broken by the enemy. This was a great <u>challenge</u>. The military finally decided to base the code on the language spoken by a Native American tribe, the Navajo. In May of 1942, the first 29 Navajo men came to <u>aid</u> the military. After they helped develop the code, they <u>accompanied</u> the soldiers overseas to help send and receive the secret messages.

Write the letter of the correct definition next to each word.

Example: ___d___ accompanied

_____ 1. aid

_____ 2. code

_____ 3. challenge

a. help or support given to someone

b. a way to use words, letters, or numbers to send secret messages

c. something difficult that you need skill or ability to do

d. went somewhere with someone

Use the academic words from the exercise above to complete the sentences.

4. My aunt _____ my class on a school trip.

5. Alex and his sister used a secret _____ to pass messages.

6. We expected an easy math test, but it was a major _____.

7. The teacher offered _____ to the students who were falling behind by helping them after class.

Complete the sentences with your own ideas.

Example: My ___*best friend*___ accompanied me to the park.

8. When I need help, _____ can offer me aid.

9. _____ sends messages in code.

10. I think the biggest challenge I face is _____.

WORD STUDY **Words with *ch* and *tch*** *Use with textbook page 73.*

> **REMEMBER** In English, the consonant clusters *ch* and *tch* sound the same but are spelled differently. For example: tou<u>ch</u> and ma<u>tch</u>. Learning these two patterns can help you spell many words correctly.

Read the words in the box below. Then write each word in the correct column in the chart.

~~chain~~	switch	attach	sketch	latch
such	watch	touch	patch	champion

Words with *-ch*	Words with *-tch*
chain	

Fill in the missing letters in each word. Use *ch* or *tch*. Check your answers in a dictionary.

Example: Mark shouldn't scra__*tch*__ his mosquito bite!

1. Cleaning my room is one of my _____ores.

2. I have to do some resear_____ on chimpanzees.

3. Risa has one _____apter left to read in the novel.

4. On Saturday, I baked a ba_____ of cookies.

5. My favorite vegetables are carrots, peas, and spina_____.

6. We usually stre_____ before and after we exercise.

REMEMBER You can skim a text to help you get a general understanding of what it is about before you read it more carefully.

Skim the paragraphs below. Answer the questions that follow.

Start Your Day with Breakfast

Breakfast is a great way to start your day because it provides energy for moving and thinking. After being inactive and sleeping for eight hours, breakfast provides you with the energy to get your day started. When you eat breakfast, your stomach breaks down food into nutrients. Your brain needs nutrients to think faster and more clearly, and your body needs them in order to be active.

Scientific research also shows that breakfast is good for your body. Researchers have found that people who skip the first meal of the day end up eating more later, which can lead to weight gain. Studies have also shown that people who eat breakfast on a regular basis have good cholesterol levels and live longer. So slow down, if only for a minute, and have something to eat before you leave your house in the morning.

1. What is the first paragraph about?

   _____

2. Read the first sentence of the next paragraph. What do you think it will be about?

   _____

3. Skim the rest of the text. Then, summarize the entire passage in one sentence.

   _____

4. What might you learn from this passage? Set a purpose for reading the passage.

   _____

5. How might skimming a passage before reading it help you to better understand the text?

   _____

COMPREHENSION   *Use with textbook page 80.*

Choose the best answer for each item. Circle the letter of the correct answer.

1. The Underground Railroad was _____.

   a. a network of people   **b.** a network of secret railroad lines   **c.** a network of tunnels

2. Harriet Tubman was nicknamed "Moses," after _____.

   a. a Biblical figure   **b.** an abolitionist leader   **c.** Union spy

3. To escape from slavery was _____.

   a. something no one tried to do   **b.** not a challenge   **c.** difficult and dangerous

4. Slavery was widespread _____.

   a. only in the South   **b.** in both the North and South   **c.** mainly in other countries

5. Runaway slaves communicated with the Underground Railroad _____.

   a. by telegram   **b.** by telephone   **c.** in secret codes

EXTENSION   *Use with textbook page 81.*

Think of a difficult challenge that you have faced. Was there someone who helped you overcome it? This person might have been a hero to you, like Harriet Tubman was to many runaway slaves. Write a few sentences about the challenge. Then write a thank you note to the person who helped you.

_____

_____

_____

_____

_____

_____

_____

GRAMMAR, USAGE, AND MECHANICS

Prepositions of Location: Where and in What Direction

Use with textbook page 82.

> **REMEMBER** Prepositions of location show where or in what direction an action occurs. A preposition is always followed by a noun or a noun phrase. Prepositions that indicate where something occurs are *in*, *at*, and *between*.
> **Example:** My grandparents' house is *in* Tucson.
> Prepositions that show direction include *to*, *from*, and *into*.
> **Example:** We walked *into* the movie theatre.

Complete each sentence below with a preposition from the box.

in	at	between	from	into

1. Harriet Tubman escaped _____ slavery.

2. When the runaways were _____ two stops on the Underground Railroad, they were in danger because they were out in the open.

3. If they were being followed, runaways might go _____ the woods.

4. Enslaved people sometimes slept _____ barns while they traveled on the Underground Railroad.

5. Runaway slaves often traveled _____ night to avoid being seen.

Read the prepositional phrases in parentheses. Use each one in a sentence.

Example: (from the chair) *The old man rose slowly from the chair.*

6. (at the fence) _____

7. (into the car) _____

8. (in the ditch) _____

9. (to the child) _____

10. (between the chimney and the bookshelf) _____

Name _____ Date _____

WRITING A NARRATIVE PARAGRAPH

Write a Story with a Starter *Use with textbook page 83.*

This is the word web that Madeline completed before writing her paragraph.

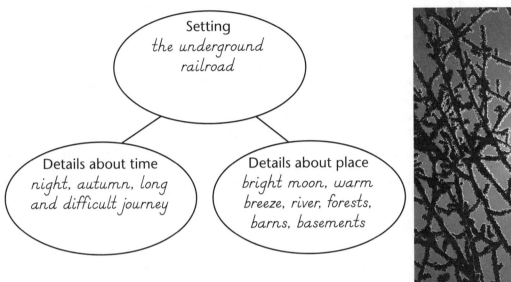

Complete your own word web with details for a fictional narrative beginning with the story starter: *The view was unlike anything I had ever seen before.*

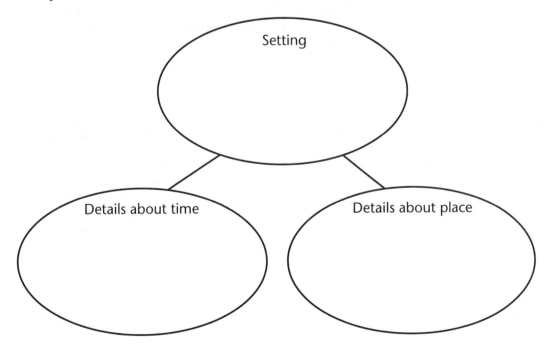

What are the benefits of facing challenges?

READING 2: "Five New Words at a Time" / "Quilt"

VOCABULARY **Literary Words** *Use with textbook page 85.*

REMEMBER **Characters** are the people or animals involved in a story. Stories are told from the **point of view** of a character or narrator. When you are reading a story, it is important to know who is telling the story. The story is told from that character's point of view. Words such as *I, our,* and *us* normally indicate a *first-person* point of view. An author's memoirs or diaries use the first-person point of view. Words such as *he, she,* and *they* normally indicate a third-person point of view. If someone who isn't in the story is telling it, the third-person point of view is used.

Label each sentence with the point of view that is used. Write the name of the character.

Point of View / Character	Sentence
third person / Norman	Norman went to the party.
1.	"Are we going?" my friend asked.
2.	"I'm tired, too," I replied.
3.	We sat down and tried to think of an answer.

Write a sentence for each character and point of view.

Character / Point of View	Sentence
Meredith: first person	*I sang the song with a smile.*
4. Samuel: third person	
5. the team: first person	

VOCABULARY **Academic Words** *Use with textbook page 86.*

Read the paragraph below. Pay attention to the underlined academic words.

> Maria is my French pen pal. We underline{communicate} mainly through e-mail. I write to her in French, and she writes to me in English. It's exciting when I get a response from her. We approach learning a foreign language in similar ways. We both like reading and writing, and we also enjoy using resources such as language CDs and videos to help with listening and pronunciation.

Write the academic words from the paragraph above next to their correct definitions.

Example: _____*response*_____: something that is said, written, or done as a reaction or reply to something else

1. _____: a supply of materials used to complete a task

2. _____: express your thoughts or feelings so other people understand them

3. _____: a way of doing something or dealing with a problem

Use the academic words from the paragraph above to complete the sentences.

4. The _____ to your letter can be found in today's newspaper.

5. Yu-Lan always used school _____, such as the library and computers.

6. I usually _____ by e-mail with my friend in Germany.

7. We tried a new _____ to solve the problem.

Complete the sentences with your own ideas.

Example: I approach tough projects ____*slowly and carefully*_____.

8. I got a positive response when I asked my friends to

_____.

9. I communicate with friends by _____.

10. Some useful resources in my town are _____.

Use with textbook page 87.

> **REMEMBER** A prefix is a letter or group of letters added to the beginning of a word to change its meaning. For example, the prefixes *im-* and *un-* mean "not." When you add *im-* to the word *possible*, the new word is *impossible*, the opposite of *possible*. Knowing just a few prefixes can help you figure out many unfamiliar words.

Look at the chart below. Add the prefixes *im-, over-, un-,* or *after-* as directed to create a new word. Write the new word on the chart. Then write the meaning.

Word	Prefix	New Word	Definition
balance	*im-*	*imbalance*	*not balanced*
1. patient	*im-*		
2. estimate	*over-*		
3. flow	*over-*		
4. even	*un-*		
5. healthy	*un-*		
6. thought	*after-*		
7. shock	*after-*		

Create a new word by adding the prefix *im-, over-, un-,* or *after-* to each word below. Write the definition next to the new word. Check a dictionary if needed.

Example: heat   *overheat   heat to excess* _____

 8. taste _____

 9. steady _____

10. effect _____

11. measurable _____

12. pay _____

13. believable _____

14. mature _____

15. look _____

READING STRATEGY IDENTIFY PROBLEMS AND SOLUTIONS

Use with textbook page 87.

> **REMEMBER** When you find the problems and solutions in a text, you will understand it better.

Read the paragraph and answer the questions that follow.

> Hannah could see that her dog, Fergus, was thirsty and hot from running in the summer sun, but she'd forgotten to bring water. She was warned that he might get overheated. Hannah made Fergus lie down, but that didn't help. Then she remembered there was a creek at the edge of the park. She took Fergus to the creek where he could get a drink of water.

1. What is the problem in the passage?

   _____

2. What is the solution in the passage?

   _____

Read the paragraph and answer the questions that follow.

> Supunnee missed her friends in Thailand, and she wouldn't be going home again for several months. She wondered what her friends were doing, and she felt sad. Then she remembered the friendly girl, Caroline, whom she'd met in class. She decided to give her a call. They made plans to meet before class for lunch. Supunnee felt much better.

3. What is the problem in the passage?

   _____

4. What is the solution in the passage?

   _____

5. How might the skill of identifying problems and solutions help you when reading a story or informational text?

   _____

Choose the best answer for each item. Circle the letter of the correct answer.

1. Yu-Lan dreaded going to school because _____.

   a. she was the smallest student

   b. she was afraid of not understanding people

   c. her mother's bad English embarrassed her

2. Yu-Lan's mother worked in a Chinese-speaking restaurant because _____.

   a. she wanted to cook Chinese food

   b. she wanted to work during the night instead of the day

   c. she didn't know much English

3. When Yu-Lan was upset, her mother _____.

   a. was cruel to her

   b. gave her confidence

   c. did not understand

4. Yu-Lan and her mother practiced English by _____.

   a. reading together

   b. going to classes together

   c. speaking English at the restaurant

5. "Quilt" is about the way families _____.

   a. seem brand-new and well put-together

   b. fall apart after many years

   c. stay together even in hard times

RESPONSE TO LITERATURE *Use with textbook page 93.*

In the poem "Quilt," Janet Wong compares the connections between her family members to the threads and fabric in a quilt. The quilt is a symbol of the love in her family. Think about your own family and friends. Write a short paragraph about a symbol that best represents the connections between you and the people you love.

_____

_____

_____

_____

_____

_____

GRAMMAR, USAGE, AND MECHANICS

Gerunds as Subjects and Objects *Use with textbook page 94.*

> **REMEMBER** A gerund is a form of a verb that can act as a noun. Gerunds are formed by adding *-ing*
> to the base form of a verb. A gerund can be the subject of a sentence or the object of a verb.
> **Examples:** *Thinking* about the test makes me nervous. I decided to stop *playing* soccer after the 8th grade.
> A gerund can also be the object of a preposition.
> **Example:** We get exercise *from running* around the track.

Complete each sentence below with the gerund of the verb in parentheses.

Example: (go) After you pass the second stop sign, keep _____*going*_____ for
two miles.

1. (surprise) _____ someone on his or her birthday is fun.

2. (memorize) _____ five words a day is a good way to learn a new
   language.

3. (say) He has a habit of _____ funny things.

4. (make) _____ breakfast will take only a few minutes.

5. (explain) The impatient teacher did not bother _____ the answers.

**Write sentences with gerunds as the subjects or objects of verbs. Use the verb in
parentheses to form the gerund.**

Example: (stand)
He tried standing on one leg for ten minutes.

6. (bicycle)

   _____

7. (travel)

   _____

8. (win)

   _____

9. (write)

   _____

10. (research)

   _____

WRITING A NARRATIVE PARAGRAPH

Rewrite a Familiar Story *Use with textbook page 95.*

This is the T-chart that Austin completed before writing his paragraph.

Yu-Lan's POV	Mother's POV
mother forced to work in a Chinese restaurant because of unfamiliarity with English	like working in a Chinese restaurant because I am able to understand others
mother never neglected us	working long hours made it difficult to spend time with my children
dreaded going to school each morning	noticed Yu-Lan seemed unhappy

Complete your own T-chart comparing different characters' points of view from a story you know well.

Name _____ Date _____

UNIT 2

What are the benefits of facing challenges?

READING 3: "The Great Fever"

VOCABULARY **Key Words** *Use with textbook page 97.*

Write each word in the box next to its definition.

| disease | experiment | fever | hypothesis | mosquitoes | virus |

Example: ____*disease*____ : an illness with specific symptoms affecting a person, animal, or plant

1. _____ : small flying biting insects that drink blood from people or animals, sometimes spreading diseases

2. _____ : a careful test you do to see how something will react in a certain situation, or to prove something is true

3. _____ : an idea that is suggested as an explanation for something, but is not yet proven to be true

4. _____ : a very small living thing that causes infectious illnesses

5. _____ : an illness in which you have a very high temperature

Use the words in the box at the top of the page to complete the sentences.

6. The scientists carried out an _____ in the chemistry lab.

7. In the garden, Lucy wears netting over her head to protect herself from

   _____ .

8. Many diseases are caused by a single _____ .

9. The doctor was very worried about the child's high _____ .

10. People with a contagious _____ should stay at home.

Read the paragraph below. Pay attention to the underlined academic words.

> Some psychologists believe that a person can <u>transmit</u> his or her mood to others. To test this <u>theory</u>, psychologists developed an experiment. The <u>objective</u> of the experiment was to see if people could transmit moods to a group. Two <u>volunteers</u> walked into a room full of people. The volunteers entered smiling and laughing. Soon, the others in the room were smiling and laughing, too!

Write the letter of the correct definition next to each word.

Example: ___b___ volunteers

_____ **1.** transmit

_____ **2.** theory

_____ **3.** objective

a. something that you are working hard to achieve

b. people who offer to do something without expecting to be paid

c. an idea that explains how something works or why something happens

d. send or pass something from one person to another

Use the academic words from the exercise above to complete the sentences.

4. The employees worked hard to reach their monthly _____.

5. All three _____ at the animal shelter were surprised when the manager offered to pay them.

6. The science experiment proved her _____.

7. The letter will _____ a message in code.

Complete the sentences with your own ideas.

Example: I believe the existence of ___*the Loch Ness Monster*___ is just a theory.

8. My main objective for the week is to _____.

9. I would like to volunteer in a _____.

10. I transmit notes to my friends by _____.

WORD STUDY Irregular Plurals *Use with textbook page 99.*

REMEMBER To make most nouns plural, add *-s* or *-es* to the end of the noun. However, some nouns are irregular and do not follow this pattern. For many singular nouns that end in consonant + *y*, change the *y* to *i* and add *-es*, as in *city—cities*. For singular nouns that end in *-is*, change the *-is* to *-es*, as in *neurosis—neuroses*.

Write the plural form of each noun.

Nouns that end in *consonant + y*		Nouns that end in *-is*	
Singular	**Plural**	**Singular**	**Plural**
Example: fly	*flies*	synthesis	*syntheses*
1. mystery		**6.** neurosis	
2. tragedy		**7.** axis	
3. memory		**8.** ellipsis	
4. opportunity		**9.** antithesis	
5. butterfly		**10.** oasis	

Write the plural form of each noun below.

Example: pony _____*ponies*_____

11. apology _____

12. parenthesis _____

13. synopsis _____

14. lady _____

15. puppy _____

Use with textbook page 99.

> **REMEMBER** Recognizing cause and effect can help you better understand a text. Look for words and phrases such as *because, since, so that, therefore,* and *as a result of.*

Read the paragraph and answer the questions that follow.

> Some students have something called test-taking anxiety. The thought of taking a test can keep them from studying well. This anxiety makes it difficult to concentrate when taking the test. Because of this nervousness, students will do poorly, even though they studied. Psychologists call it test anxiety and offer students tips on dealing with their feelings, so that they can perform better during tests.

1. What is the cause in the paragraph?

   _____

2. What is the effect in the paragraph?

   _____

Read the paragraph and answer the questions that follow.

> Javan was excited about going camping. He became disappointed when the bus had to stop at the bridge. The river was high and flooded the bridge, so they couldn't get across to the campgrounds. As a result, the group got off the bus and crossed the river on foot in a place where the water was low. They hiked the rest of the way to the campsite.

3. What is the cause in the paragraph?

   _____

4. What is the effect in the paragraph?

   _____

5. How might the skill of identifying cause and effect help you when reading the text?

   _____

   _____

COMPREHENSION *Use with textbook page 104.*

Choose the best answer for each item. Circle the letter of the correct answer.

1. Yellow fever was feared because many people died from it and because _____.

   a. it led to more serious diseases

   b. it caused great suffering

   c. it caused people's skin to turn blue

2. Yellow fever got its name _____.

   a. because victims' skin and eyes turned yellow

   b. because victims liked yellow

   c. because yellow pills seemed to help cure the disease

3. Finlay believed that yellow fever is transmitted by _____.

   a. mosquitoes

   b. warm, damp air

   c. polluted water

4. Finlay created a map that showed that mosquito habitats and yellow fever epidemics were _____.

   a. in different seasons

   b. in the same places

   c. in very different places

5. In the 1930s, a vaccine was created to _____.

   a. kill mosquito eggs

   b. prevent jaundice

   c. prevent yellow fever

EXTENSION *Use with textbook page 105.*

Research five diseases. For each, note when it was discovered and tell when a cure was found or a vaccine was developed. If no cure or vaccine exists, note that as well.

Disease	Disease Discovered	Cure Found or Vaccine Developed
influenza	400 B.C.E.	1944

GRAMMAR, USAGE, AND MECHANICS

Passive Voice: Simple Past; Regular and Irregular Past Participles

Use with textbook page 106.

> **REMEMBER** Use the passive voice when the focus is on the receiver, not the performer, of an action.
> A *by*-phrase identifies the performer. **Example:** The election was won by the best candidate.
> Form the passive voice with the verb *be* + the past participle. Regular past participles are formed by
> adding *-d* or *-ed* to the base form of the verb. Irregular past participles must be memorized.
> **Example:** The cookies were eaten at the end of the club meeting.

Complete each sentence with the passive form of the verb in parentheses.

Example: (impress) The scientists ___*were impressed*___ by Finlay's theory.

1. (know) Yellow fever _____ as yellow jack.

2. (kill) Troops _____ by the deadly virus.

3. (study) Mosquitoes _____ by Dr. Carlos Finlay.

4. (train) Dr. Walter Reed _____ in the study of bacteria.

5. (find) No cure for yellow fever _____.

Rewrite each sentence using the passive voice.

Example: Ships carried the immature mosquitoes from Africa to America.

The immature mosquitoes were carried by ships from Africa to America.

6. Doctors and scientists read accounts of yellow fever.

_____

7. Yellow fever claimed millions of lives.

_____

8. Yellow fever struck the Mississippi Valley.

_____

9. The researchers proved the doctor's theory.

_____

10. Vaccines controlled yellow fever.

_____

Name _____ Date _____

WRITING A NARRATIVE PARAGRAPH

Write a Personal Narrative *Use with textbook page 107.*

This is the three-column chart that Ari completed before writing his paragraph.

Who was there	What happened	What was said
my mother and I	I had the flu.	"Oh my gosh! You're as pale as a ghost! What's wrong?!"

Complete your own three-column chart for a personal narrative about a memorable experience you had with a friend or classmate.

Who was there	What happened	What was said

UNIT 2

What are the benefits of facing challenges?

READING 4: "An Interview with Gary Paulsen" / From *Hatchet*

VOCABULARY **Literary Words** *Use with textbook page 109.*

> **REMEMBER** An **author's influences** are factors that may affect his or her writing. These include personal experiences, culture, and world events. An **external conflict** is a struggle between a character and some kind of outside force. This can be another person or a force of nature.

Read each sentence. Write *yes* if it depicts an external conflict. Write *no* if it does not depict an external conflict.

External?	Description
no	Tom wanted a cup of coffee very badly.
1.	Paolo struggled to cross the stream without falling.
2.	She didn't think she could get past the mean guard dog.
3.	I woke up angry today.
4.	Agi's father always tells her what to do.
5.	The rain made us all wet and cold.

Read the brief author interview below. Circle the author influences that are discussed in the interview.

Q: Have your experiences affected your writing at all?

A: Yes, I moved to Chicago from rural Ohio when I was twenty. The move was difficult for me, but I came to love the city. My favorite setting for my stories is Chicago, and my characters often struggle with the hardships of city life. It is easy to meet people in the city, and I had many good friends who helped me. Often my characters will find someone who similarly helps them. The lessons I have learned from people I admire are more important to me than writing about favorite places or things.

VOCABULARY **Academic Words** *Use with textbook page 110.*

Read the paragraph below. Pay attention to the underlined academic words.

> The rivers of the northwestern United States are home to millions of salmon. Salmon need to travel up and down the rivers to <u>survive</u>. Unfortunately, many of these rivers are blocked by dams. Each <u>structure</u> creates lakes and helps make fresh water <u>available</u> to humans. However, the dams also block the salmon's path and have <u>injured</u> or killed many salmon as they try to pass through them.

Write the academic words from the paragraph above next to their correct definitions.

Example: ___*available*___ : able to be used or seen

1. _____: continue to live after an accident or illness

2. _____: hurt

3. _____: a building or something that has been built

Use the academic words from the paragraph above to complete the sentences.

4. We were surprised that no one was _____ in the crash.

5. I'm not _____ to talk during lunchtime.

6. If you were lost in the woods, would it be possible to _____ on water and berries?

7. Turn right at the giant steel _____ being built in the middle of town.

Complete the sentences with your own ideas.

Example: I want to survive to the age of _____*250*_____.

8. The _____ is a famous structure in our town.

9. In our school library, _____ are available as resources to help students learn.

10. If you're not careful, you can get injured while _____.

REMEMBER A compound noun is made up of two or more nouns. Compound nouns can be written in different ways. A closed compound noun is written as one word, as in *sailboat*.

Look at the nouns in the boxes below. Then combine the nouns in each row to make a closed compound noun.

Noun	+ Noun	= Compound Noun
stock	broker	*stockbroker*
1. sales	person	
2. data	base	
3. tooth	paste	
4. black	board	
5. sea	port	

Create closed compound nouns by combining the nouns in the box. Then use each closed compound noun in a sentence. Note that nouns may be used more that once.

burn	bed	coat	room	beam	drop	rain	fall	sun	dial

Example: *bed + room = bedroom   We painted the bedroom white.*

6. _____

7. _____

8. _____

9. _____

10. _____

READING STRATEGY **PREDICT** *Use with textbook page 111.*

REMEMBER Before you read, predict what a story will be about. You can also make new predictions as you read. Stop from time to time and ask, "What will happen next?" Look for clues in the story. Think about what you already know.

Read the paragraph and answer the questions that follow.

Seeing Stefan Again

One Saturday morning Angela and her two cousins were riding the subway downtown to the New York Public Library to do research. Two stops before they were going to get off, Angela saw Stefan waiting on a subway platform. She shouted "Stefan!" just before the subway doors closed. He turned just in time to see her before the train left the stop. When they reached the public library stop, Angela got off the train and stood on the platform, stunned she had seen him in the city. She was still standing there when the next train arrived and Stefan stepped through the sliding doors.

1. Read the title. What do you predict the story will be about?

   _____

2. Where does the story happen?

   _____

3. When does the story happen?

   _____

4. After you read the paragraph, what do you predict will happen next?

   _____

5. Set a purpose for reading this text.

   _____

COMPREHENSION   *Use with textbook page 120.*

Choose the best answer for each item. Circle the letter of the correct answer.

1. Gary Paulsen's childhood was _____.

   a. difficult for him   **b.** boring for him   **c.** enjoyable for him

2. As an adult, Paulsen has reacted to his childhood by _____.

   a. trying to forget it   **b.** writing about it   **c.** going back to where
                                                                      he grew up

3. Brian, the character in "Hatchet," is _____.

   a. like the author,   **b.** not like the author,   **c.** a pilot in Canada
       Gary Paulsen   Gary Paulsen

4. Brian is a(n) _____.

   a. mean person   **b.** scared person   **c.** adventuresome person

5. Gary Paulsen says the best thing for young writers is to _____.

   a. write alone   **b.** only read poetry   **c.** read all the time

RESPONSE to LITERATURE   *Use with textbook page 121.*

Gary Paulsen drew on his own childhood to create the story *Hatchet*. Find a paragraph or image that you like very much in *Hatchet*. Draw a picture illustrating the paragraph or image.

GRAMMAR, USAGE, AND MECHANICS

Simple and Compound Sentences *Use with textbook page 122.*

> **REMEMBER** A simple sentence contains a subject and a predicate. The predicate tells what the subject does. A predicate always has a verb. **Example:** I walk my dog after school.
> A compound sentence has two simple sentences joined by a coordinating conjunction (*and, but, or,* or *so*), so it often has two verbs. Use a comma before the conjunction that joins the two sentences.
> **Example:** I swim after school, and sometimes I play soccer.

Write *simple* if a sentence is simple. Write *compound* if it is compound.

_____ **1.** Birds and butterflies fly south in the fall.

_____ **2.** The sun rises in the east, and it sets in the west.

_____ **3.** Spending time in the woods or by the ocean teaches you about nature.

_____ **4.** Dragonflies migrate, but they fly in only one direction.

_____ **5.** I became interested in Gary Paulsen, so now I want to read more of his books.

Write compound sentences by adding the coordinating conjunction in parentheses and a simple sentence to each sentence below.

Example: (and) Bees were buzzing, *and in the distance a crow was cawing.*

 6. (but) They planted a garden, _____

 7. (and) She went for a walk in the woods, _____

 8. (or) Tomorrow he will build a tree house, _____

 9. (so) It was getting cold, _____

10. (but) It has not rained all week, _____

WRITING A NARRATIVE PARAGRAPH

Write a Personal Letter *Use with textbook page 123.*

This is the graphic organizer that George completed before writing his paragraph.

(Date)
October 1, 2009

(Salutation
or greeting)
Dear Joe,

(Body)
I went on a camping trip with my cousins.
It took us almost six hours to get to the campsite.
We put up the tent and it rained.
The next day, we hiked to the other side of the mountain.

(Closing,) *Best,*
(Signature) *George*

Complete your own graphic organizer for a letter to a friend or relative about a memorable event you've experienced.

EDIT AND PROOFREAD   *Use with textbook page 130.*

Read the paragraph below carefully. Look for mistakes in spelling, punctuation, and grammar. Mark the mistakes with proofreader's marks (textbook page 460). Then rewrite the paragraph correctly on the lines below.

Last summer, I go away to a nearby college as part of a program for high school students. I took one class in chemistry and one in english. The classes was harder than my high school classes, but I worked hard and did well. the students in my program all stayd in the same dormitory We played soccer in the hallway! The athletic field was Nearby, but it wasn't close enough. Visiting the city was fun, too. I had never had a chance to exploar such a big city on my own. I road my bike at musuems and shops, and my new friends and I walked on the waterfront at night. I enjoyed studying for classes and working with professors But I enjoyed my new freedom even more.

Underline the vocabulary items you know and can use well. Review and practice any you haven't underlined. Underline them when you know them well.

Literary Words	Key Words	Academic Words	
characters	fugitive	accompanied	available
point of view	heritage	aid	injured
author's influences	network	challenge	structure
external conflict	runaway	code	survive
	shelter	approach	
	Underground Railroad	communicate	
	disease	resources	
	experiment	response	
	fever	objective	
	hypothesis	theory	
	mosquitoes	transmit	
	virus	volunteers	

Put a check by the skills you can perform well. Review and practice any you haven't checked off. Check them off when you can perform them well.

Skills	I can . . .
Word Study	☐ spell words using *ch* and *tch*. ☐ recognize and use prefixes *im-*, *over-*, *un-*, *after-*. ☐ recognize and use irregular plurals. ☐ recognize and use closed compound nouns.
Reading Strategies	☐ skim. ☐ identify problems and solutions. ☐ recognize cause and effect. ☐ predict.
Grammar, Usage, and Mechanics	☐ use prepositions of location: where and in what direction. ☐ use gerunds as subjects and objects. ☐ use the passive voice in the simple past; with regular and irregular past participles. ☐ use simple and compound sentences.
Writing	☐ write a story with a starter. ☐ rewrite a familiar story. ☐ write a personal narrative. ☐ write a personal letter. ☐ write a fictional narrative.

Name _____ Date _____

Learn about Art with the Smithsonian
American Art Museum *Use with textbook pages 132–133.*

LEARNING TO LOOK

Look at *The Sick Child* by J. Bond Francisco on page 133 in your textbook. Study the
hands of the boy and the woman sitting beside him. Write three details about the
boy's hands and the clown that he holds. State facts, not opinions.

Boy's Hands

Example: _He holds the clown by the leg._____

1. _____

2. _____

3. _____

Write three details about the woman's hands and the knitting needles she's
working with.

Woman's Hands

4. _____

5. _____

6. _____

INTERPRETATION

Look at *The Sick Child* again. What might the woman be thinking? Write your
answers below.

Example: _If only his fever would break, he would get well quickly!_____

_____

_____

_____

_____

_____

_____

Look at *Embroidered Garment* by Alice Eugenia Ligon on page 132 in your textbook.
Use the artwork to complete the KWLH chart below.

K	W	L	H
What do you **know** about this work of art?	What do you **want** to learn about how the artist made it?	What have you **learned** about the artist and her work?	**How** did you learn this?
		She is a woman.	

Name _____ Date _____

How are relationships with others important?

READING 1: From *Salsa Stories* "Aguinaldo"

VOCABULARY **Literary Words** *Use with textbook page 137.*

REMEMBER **Irony** is the difference between what happens and what a reader expects to happen in a story. Ironic situations can cause surprise and amusement. **Foreshadowing** is an author's use of clues to hint at what might happen later in a story. It builds suspense and shapes the reader's expectations.

Read the description of each situation. Write *irony* if it is an example of irony. Write *foreshadowing* if it is an example of foreshadowing.

Irony or foreshadowing?	Situation
foreshadowing	It was an unusually icy day when they began their car trip. The roads were slippery.
1.	Jeffrey drove for four straight days – only to end up back where he started.
2.	The policeman watched the customer with interest. Then he picked up his radio and said, "Chief, could you check on something for me?"
3.	Our team did well that day. But there were a lot of games left, and things didn't go well for very long . . .

Read the passage. Underline the elements of foreshadowing in the story.

Miles threw his shoes and shirt into the closet carelessly. He looked down at his desk. There was an unopened letter sitting there, but he tried not to look at it. He opened the window, then shut it again for no reason. The clock seemed to tick more loudly than before. He looked at the picture of his family hanging on the wall. *What if it's bad news?* he thought. He went downstairs for a glass of water, but once he got to the kitchen he forgot to pour it. He thought of his brother, and how much time had passed since his previous letter. Why would he write now? A moment passed. "OK then," Miles said. He marched upstairs, ready for anything. Even bad news.

4. What do you think happens next? _____

Read the paragraph below. Pay attention to the underlined academic words.

There is a non-profit organization in our town that <u>distributes</u> free lunches to the elderly. Volunteers bring the lunches to elderly <u>residents</u>' homes every day at noon. No elderly person who requests a free lunch is ever <u>rejected</u>. Both volunteers and the elderly find delivering and receiving free lunches a very <u>positive</u> experience.

Write the letter of the correct definition next to each word.

Example: ___*b*___ rejected

_____ **1.** residents

_____ **2.** distributes

_____ **3.** positive

a. gives something to different people or places

b. decided not to do something

c. good or useful

d. people who live in a place

Use the academic words from the exercise above to complete the sentences.

4. Even though the situation was unpleasant, she tried to keep a

_____ attitude.

5. All the _____ of the apartment building helped to keep the grounds clean.

6. He _____ the man's offer of payment when he saw how poor the man was.

7. Every Sunday she _____ flyers to her neighbors to advertise her crafts store.

Complete the sentences with your own ideas.

Example: I had a very positive experience while ___*volunteering at the soup kitchen*___.

8. If I ask a friend to go out for the evening and am rejected, I usually feel

_____.

9. I like the residents of my neighborhood because _____.

10. Before each class, my teacher distributes _____.

WORD STUDY **Spelling s- Blends** *Use with textbook page 139.*

> **REMEMBER** A consonant blend is two or three consonants that are placed together in a word. You can hear the sound of each consonant in a consonant blend.

Look at the words in the word box. Underline the consonant blend that begins each word. Then write each word in the correct category in the chart.

| sport | stall | strength | <u>sw</u>ing | spell | stand | strange | swell | spend | store |

sw-	sp-	st-	str-
swing			

Complete each sentence by adding the correct s- blend in the space provided.

1. I want to _____**end** more time at home.

2. My favorite _____**ort** is soccer.

3. I have to stay in bed so that I can recover my _____**ength**.

4. I do not know how to _____**ell** that word.

5. It was a very _____**ange** movie.

6. I have a _____**omachache**.

7. My parents always make me feel _____**ecial**.

8. I am going to the _____**ore** to buy milk.

Use with textbook page 139.

REMEMBER Analyzing the cultural context of a story helps you visualize and understand what's happening. Notice the author's descriptions and think about the characters' language, country, ideas, and beliefs. Also, think of what you know from your own experiences.

Read each paragraph and answer the questions that follow.

I didn't know what to expect when David invited me to his Chanukah party. He explained that Chanukah was the Jewish festival of lights. We played a game with a four-sided top called a dreidel to win the most Chanukah gelt—foil-wrapped chocolate candy. Later, he and his family lit a special candleholder called a menorah. We had delicious potato pancakes called latkes and later we had special Chanukah doughnuts called sufganiot. Yum!

1. What culture does the narrator experience?

_____

2. What does the narrator learn about the culture of the family he or she visits?

_____

_____

3. How does the family in this passage feel about their culture?

_____

_____

4. Did you learn anything new about Chanukah from this passage?

_____

_____

5. How do you think the strategy of recognizing a story's cultural context can help you read with better comprehension?

_____

_____

COMPREHENSION   *Use with textbook page 148.*

Choose the best answer for each item. Circle the letter of the correct answer.

1. Marilia doesn't want to go on the trip to the nursing home because _____.

   a. she is sick   **b.** her grandmother died in one   **c.** nursing homes are boring

2. An *aguinaldo* is a _____.

   a. nursing home patient   **b.** coconut sweet   **c.** surprise Christmas gift

3. The morning of the trip, Marilia _____.

   a. is excited   **b.** refuses to leave home   **c.** pretends to be sick

4. During her time with Elenita, Marilia feels _____.

   a. happy   **b.** angry   **c.** bored

5. The main irony of the story is that Marilia _____.

   a. spoke to an elderly woman   **b.** tried to escape her obligations but couldn't   **c.** received an *aguinaldo* of her own

RESPONSE TO LITERATURE   *Use with textbook page 149.*

By the end of the story, Marilia has made a new friend. If the story continues, and Marilia visits the nursing home again, what do you think will happen?

_____

_____

_____

_____

_____

GRAMMAR, USAGE, AND MECHANICS

Imperatives *Use with textbook page 150.*

> **REMEMBER** Imperatives are often used to give instructions. Imperatives are formed with the base form of the verb. The subject *you* is implied but is not actually said or written.
> **Example:** *Turn on* the oven.
> To make the negative form of an imperative add *don't* before the base form of the verb.
> **Example:** *Don't touch* a hot plate.

Underline all the imperatives, and circle all the negative imperatives in the recipe.

> Preheat oven to 360 degrees. Mix butter, eggs and sugar until foamy. Slowly add flour to butter-egg-sugar mixture. In a separate bowl, stir cocoa into a third of the dough. Don't use all the cocoa. Now it is time to pour the dough into the baking pan, alternating layers of light and dark dough. Use a fork to create a pattern. Place the baking pan into the preheated oven.

Rewrite each sentence using an imperative.

Example: You need to use two pieces of bread.

   Use two pieces of bread.

1. First you need to use a knife to put peanut butter on both slices.

   _____

2. Then you should spread the jelly evenly on both slices of bread.

   _____

3. After that, you need to put one slice of bread on top of the other.

   _____

4. Next it is time to cut the sandwich in half diagonally.

   _____

5. Now you can enjoy your sandwich.

   _____

WRITING AN EXPOSITORY PARAGRAPH

Write Instructions *Use with textbook page 151.*

This is the sequence chart that Haley completed before writing her paragraph.

> **First**
> *Do an Internet search with the key word <u>volunteer</u> and your zip code.*

> **Then**
> *Collect information about each place that interests you.*

> **Next**
> *Call your friends and ask them if they are interested in volunteering.*

> **Finally**
> *Choose a place to volunteer and call or visit them to find out more.*

Complete your own sequence chart containing instructions for something you know how to do well.

> **First**

> **Then**

> **Next**

> **Finally**

How are relationships with others important?

READING 2: "Sowing the Seeds of Peace" / "Seeds of Peace: Cultivating Friendships"

VOCABULARY **Key Words** *Use with textbook page 153.*

Write each word in the box next to its definition.

barriers	confrontation	cultivate	enemies	political	violence

Example: ___*enemies*___: people who hate you or want to harm you

1. _____: relating to the government of a country

2. _____: try to develop a friendship with someone who can help you

3. _____: things that prevent people from doing something

4. _____: an argument or fight

5. _____: behavior that is intended to hurt other people physically

Use the words in the box at the top of the page to complete the sentences.

6. The government wants to keep any of its _____ from getting too strong.

7. It's good to _____ friendships with people who share your interests.

8. Their _____ differences led to an argument about government.

9. They cannot seem to stop fighting: every time they see each other, there's a

   _____.

10. _____ is not the way to solve a problem, because we should try to solve things peacefully.

VOCABULARY **Academic Words** *Use with textbook page 154.*

Read the paragraph below. Pay attention to the underlined academic words.

> When I first met Sanaya, I <u>assumed</u> we could never be friends. She wore very strange clothes and her hair was dyed pink. But I remembered what my mother always said: "Don't judge a book by its cover." One shouldn't just <u>focus</u> on appearance. We are all <u>individuals</u> and each person has value. So I decided that if I just tried talking to Sanaya, maybe I would like her. I was right! We discovered we had many <u>similarities</u>. Now she is my best friend.

Write the academic words from the paragraph above next to their correct definitions.

Example: _____*focus*_____ : pay special attention to a particular person or thing instead of others

1. _____ : the qualities of being similar, or the same

2. _____ : thought that something was true without having proof

3. _____ : people; not a whole group

Use the academic words from the paragraph above to complete the sentences.

4. The students preferred to receive their diplomas one at a time, as

   _____.

5. The student _____ he had done well on the test, but he was wrong.

6. The girls learned that their _____ were as important as their differences.

7. This week in history class we will _____ on the War of the Roses.

Complete the sentences with your own ideas.

Example: Two similarities between my friend and me are
   _____*our tempers and our interest in history*_____ .

8. After school I like to focus on _____.

9. For a long time, I assumed that _____.

10. I think that it's important for people to be treated as individuals because

   _____.

> **REMEMBER** A suffix is a letter or group of letters placed at the end of a base word. Adding a suffix changes the meaning of the base word. Adding the suffix *-er* or *-or* to a base word adds the meaning "one who." **Example:** *Traveler* means "one who travels."

Look at the base words and suffixes in the chart. Add the suffix *-er* or *-or* to create a new word. Then write the definition of the new word.

teach	sing	play	facilitate	create	visit	act	read	write	own

Base Word	+ Suffix	= New Word	Definition
write	-er	*writer*	*one who writes*
1. instruct	-or		
2. perform	-er		
3. inspect	-or		
4. believe	-er		
5. create	-or		
6. review	-er		
7. edit	-or		
8. direct	-or		

Complete each sentence by adding *-er* or *-or* in the space provided. Use a dictionary if needed.

9. The act_____ was great in his role as a spy.

10. Diego is the best play_____ on our soccer team.

11. The artist was a brilliant sculpt_____.

12. My mother is the own _____ of a business.

13. We have a visit _____ at our school today.

14. Mr. Jones is my favorite teach _____.

15. I'd like to be a photograph _____.

READING STRATEGY | COMPARE AND CONTRAST

Use with textbook page 155.

> **REMEMBER** When you compare, you see how things are similar. When you contrast, you see how things are different. Comparing and contrasting can help you understand what you read.

Read each paragraph. Then answer the questions that follow.

Dara and Dora are identical twins. They look the same with dark hair and big brown eyes. Their friends call them opposites, however. Dara is smart but grumpy. Dora is pleasant but lazy.

1. How are Dara and Dora alike?

   _____

   _____

2. How are Dara and Dora different?

   _____

   _____

The United Kingdom and the United States have a lot in common. English is the first language in both countries. Both countries have been the most powerful nations in the world. However, the United Kingdom is small and the United States is large. In the U.K., people love soccer, rugby and cricket; in the U.S. they favor football, basketball, and baseball—although soccer is becoming more popular than ever.

3. How are the United States and the United Kingdom alike?

   _____

   _____

4. What are some differences between the United Kingdom and the United States?

   _____

   _____

5. How can comparing and contrasting make you a better reader?

   _____

   _____

Choose the best answer for each item. Circle the letter of the correct answer.

1. The purpose of Seeds of Peace is to _____.

   a. teach people how to argue about politics and religion

   b. help bring understanding to the Middle East

   c. perform research on kids

2. Seeds of Peace combines regular camp activities with _____.

   a. two-hour "coexistence sessions"

   b. international competitions

   c. history lessons about Palestine and Israel

3. In the bunk, the girls argue about _____.

   a. tourism in Jerusalem

   b. which religion is better and more ancient

   c. control of the city of Jerusalem

4. The article asks you to compare and contrast the views of _____.

   a. Middle Eastern children

   b. students and counselors

   c. children and politicians

5. Both Eitan and Marisa imply that they are happy that _____.

   a. they learned about rowing in canoes

   b. they got time off from school

   c. they made new friends

EXTENSION *Use with textbook page 161.*

Look up five areas of the world where conflict and war are ongoing. Who is involved in each conflict? How long has it gone on? Write the results of your research in the chart.

Location	Who is involved?	How long?
Iraq	Sunnis, Shiites, Kurds, United States	since 2003

GRAMMAR, USAGE, AND MECHANICS

Independent and Dependent Clauses *Use with textbook page 162.*

> **REMEMBER** An independent clause consists of at least a subject and a verb, and expresses a complete thought. The conjunctions *but, and, yet, or,* or *so* join two independent clauses. A dependent clause consists of a subject and a verb, but it does NOT express a complete thought. A dependent clause must be connected to an independent clause by conjunctions such as *because, before,* or *as.*

Underline all independent clauses and circle all dependent clauses in each sentence. Note that a sentence may contain two independent clauses.

Example: (When Noor joined the camp,) he didn't know that he would meet Shirlee.

1. At the camp, Arabs and Israelis meet for the first time and they learn to get along.

2. Sometimes the campers fight with each other because they disagree.

3. Arabs and Israelis disagree on many topics, and Jerusalem is probably the one they disagree on the most.

4. Arabs feel they have a historic right to the city, but Israelis feel the same.

5. Before Seeds of Peace, many children would not have been friends.

Join the clauses with the conjunction in parentheses.

6. (because) The camp was amazing. I learned a lot about the world.

   _____

7. (before) The situation got out of control. The counselors would help us talk about the issues.

   _____

8. (but) Many of our discussions were heated. We never got angry at each other.

   _____

9. (because) I made new friends. There were so many interesting people.

   _____

10. (so) I will tell my friends about Seeds of Peace. They will join next year.

    _____

WRITING AN EXPOSITORY PARAGRAPH

Write a Critique *Use with textbook page 163.*

This is the concept web that Nicole completed before writing her paragraph.

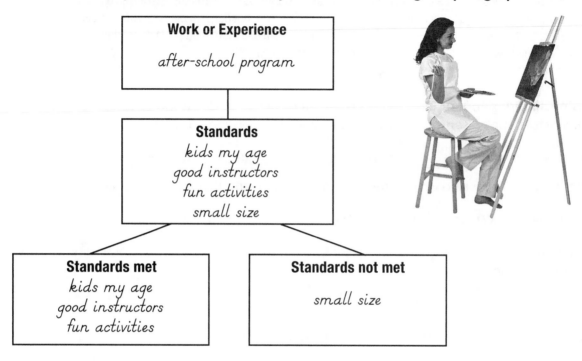

Complete your own content web with ideas for a critique of a story, movie, video game, or place you have visited.

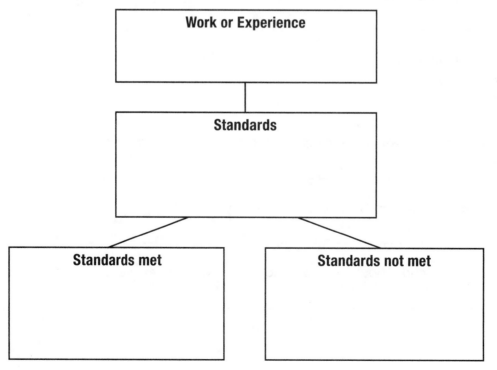

UNIT 3

How are relationships with others important?

READING 3: From *Blue Willow*

VOCABULARY **Literary Words** *Use with textbook page 165.*

> **REMEMBER** **Oral tradition** is the practice of storytellers passing stories down from one generation to the next. These stories sometimes included a **legend**, or traditional story that moves away from factual events to describe more fictional events and characters. A **character motive** is a reason that explains a character's thoughts, feelings, action, and speech.

For each situation listed, give the motivation of the main character.

Motivation	Situation
fatigue	Luke put down the ax and wiped his brow. Almost done, he thought, and then I can finally go to sleep!
1.	"I don't want to see it," Deng said. He backed away from the display slowly, shaking. "It's too awful to even think about," he added.
2.	DeWayne looked greedily at the stack of $20 bills that would be given out as prizes. He grinned and rubbed his hands. "I'd like to enter the contest," he said.
3.	Corrina looked at the clock every few minutes. When the day was over, her parents would arrive. If she could have made time move faster by working harder, she would have.

Does one of the passages have the characteristics of a legend? Write *yes* or *no*.

4. _____ Thor raised his hammer and struck the earth to scare away the fiery dragon. Behind the dragon he could see treasure boxes spilling over with gold.

5. _____ The weather in Miami, Florida, is often humid and hot. Even in the winter, the temperatures can be in the high 70s and low 80s.

Read the paragraph below. Pay attention to the underlined academic words.

John's uncle is an <u>authoritative</u> figure among the Dagomba people of northern Ghana. He is a griot—someone who tells stories through music. John had always wanted to visit him. Last month, after getting the <u>consent</u> of his uncle, John's parents surprised him with a plane ticket to Ghana. His <u>reaction</u> was pure excitement. John spent two weeks in Ghana and his uncle taught him how to play a "talking drum." John's <u>encounter</u> with his uncle was one he will never forget.

Write the letter of the correct definition next to each word.

Example: ___c___ reaction

_____ 1. authoritative

_____ 2. encounter

_____ 3. consent

a. respected and trusted as being true, or making people respect or obey you

b. an occasion when you meet someone without planning to

c. the way you behave in response to someone or something

d. permission to do something

Use the academic words from the exercise above to complete the sentences.

4. The forest ranger had an unexpected _____ with a grizzly bear.

5. The students all had a positive _____ to the field-trip announcement.

6. Before the operation could begin, the patient had to give her _____.

7. This article contains several mistakes, so it is not an _____ source.

Complete the sentences with your own ideas.

Example: ___The Senator___ is an authoritative leader.

8. When I get bad news, my reaction can range from

_____ to _____.

9. I need parental consent before I can _____.

10. I once had a funny encounter with _____.

WORD STUDY **Synonyms** *Use with textbook page 167.*

REMEMBER Synonyms are words that have the same or nearly the same meaning.
Example: *loud* and *noisy*

For each word in column 1, find its synonym in column 2. Write the letter of the synonym next to each word.

1. pretty _____   **a.** costly

2. kind _____   **b.** cruel

3. mean _____   **c.** nice

4. large _____   **d.** attractive

5. expensive _____   **e.** big

For each of the words below, write a synonym. Use a thesaurus or dictionary if needed.

6. ask _____

7. inform _____

8. knowledge _____

9. shout _____

10. detest _____

11. beautiful _____

12. small _____

13. clever _____

14. unusual _____

15. cheap _____

Use with textbook page 167.

> **REMEMBER** When you identify with a character, you try to understand the actions and feelings of a character. This can help you enjoy and understand a story.

Read each paragraph. Then answer the questions that follow.

Martina saw that Grayson had left his social studies test right on the library table. Nobody else was around. If she wanted to, she could take a quick look at his answers. After all, Grayson was the most brilliant student in the class. Martina hadn't taken the test herself. But on the other hand, what would Grandma Rose think if she found out that her granddaughter was a cheater? *I need a good grade!* she thought. *What should I do?*

1. What choice is Martina facing in this passage?

_____

2. What would you do if you were Martina, and why?

_____

_____

Zach loved creating music. He played guitar, drums, and piano, and recorded his songs on his computer. He knew they were getting better all the time. However he had a problem: when he opened his mouth to sing, he was always off-key. Then he learned about the band contest. The winner could get a scholarship to music school. It was everything he dreamed about. How could he show how good his music was when he couldn't sing?

3. What does the main character care about in this passage?

_____

4. What problem does Zach face in this passage?

_____

_____

5. How can the strategy of identifying with a character help you become a better reader?

_____

_____

Name _____ Date _____

Choose the best answer for each item. Circle the letter of the correct answer.

1. Kung Shi Fair and Chang the Good _____.

   a. never meet   **b.** are sworn enemies   **c.** fall in love
       in the story

2. The merchant attempts to _____.

   a. keep Kung Shi Fair   **b.** scare the villagers   **c.** bring people together
       and Chang the   with stories about
       Good apart   a ferocious leopard

3. Kung Shi Fair and Chang believe that _____.

   a. they will kill   **b.** one day they   **c.** the merchant will bring
       the leopard   will marry   them gifts

4. The merchant insists that Kung Shi Fair wait for _____.

   a. two swallows   **b.** a rainbow   **c.** a bolt of lightning

5. If the merchant had not been so stubborn, then perhaps _____.

   a. his daughter would   **b.** he would have caught   **c.** Chang might never have
       have lived   the leopard   met Kung Shi Fair

RESPONSE TO LITERATURE *Use with textbook page 177.*

Write a different ending to the story *Blue Willow*. Tell what might have happened if Kung Shi Fair's father had approved of the poor fisherman.

_____

_____

_____

_____

_____

GRAMMAR, USAGE, AND MECHANICS

Expressions to Compare and Contrast *Use with textbook page 178.*

> **REMEMBER** To compare ideas, use *and so* and *and . . . too*. If the verb *be* is used in one half of the
> sentence, it should be used in the other.
> **Example:** The apples were delicious, and so were the blueberries.
> When other verbs are used in the first half of the sentence, use a form of *do* in the second half.
> **Example:** She cheered for the musicians, and so did I.
> To contrast ideas, use *but . . . not* and *and yet . . .*
> **Example:** We wanted to see the movie, and yet we never had time.

Underline the expressions used to compare and contrast in the sentences.

Example: She loved swimming, <u>but</u> he did not like the beach.

1. I like apple picking, and so does my dad.

2. My grandmother needed to stop and rest, and we did, too!

3. This park is big, but it's not as big as the other one.

4. It was quite late, and yet the sky was still bright.

5. Fernando was quite tired, and so was Armando.

Complete the sentences with words from the box.

and . . . is, too	and . . . does, too	but . . . is not	but . . . does not
and yet	and so does	and so is	

6. The weather in California is warm, _____ the weather in Iceland

   _____.

7. I liked the movie, _____ I thought it was a little dull.

8. I love lacrosse, _____ Miguel.

9. New York is a large city, _____ London _____.

10. China is very interesting, _____ Japan.

WRITING AN EXPOSITORY PARAGRAPH

Write to Compare and Contrast *Use with textbook page 179.*

This is the Venn diagram that Austin completed before writing his paragraph.

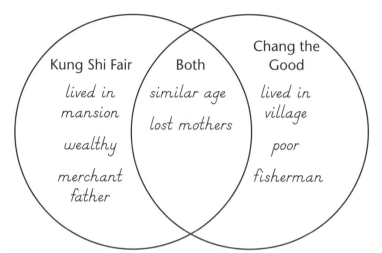

Kung Shi Fair

lived in mansion

wealthy

merchant father

Both

similar age

lost mothers

Chang the Good

lived in village

poor

fisherman

Complete your own Venn diagram comparing and contrasting two people, places, or things you know well.

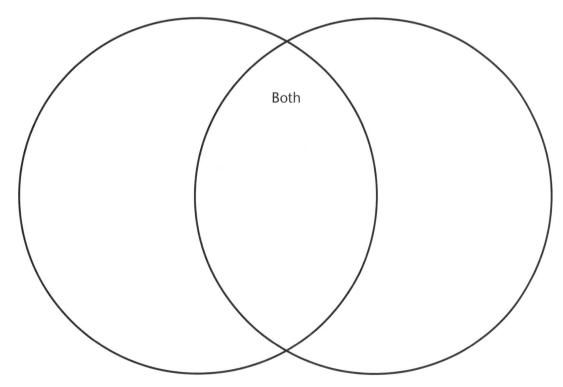

Both

How are relationships with others important?

READING 4: "Partnerships in Nature"

VOCABULARY Key Words *Use with textbook page 181.*

Write each word in the box next to its definition.

commensal	mutualistic	nature	parasites	protection	symbiosis

Example: ___*parasites*___ : organisms that live on or in other organisms and harm them while getting food from them

1. _____ : defense against harm

2. _____ : a partnership that benefits both partners

3. _____ : everything in the world not made or controlled by humans

4. _____ : partnerships between species

5. _____ : a relationship in which one species is helped and one is unharmed

Use the words in the box at the top of the page to complete the sentences.

6. _____ such as bacteria pose a threat to humans.

7. A tree can provide _____ from the rain.

8. In a _____ relationship, both partners benefit.

9. In _____, an organism's survival often depends on its ability to form relationships.

10. A tree providing shade to a bird is an example of a _____ relationship.

VOCABULARY **Academic Words** *Use with textbook page 182.*

Read the paragraph below. Pay attention to the underlined academic words.

> Many species <u>interact</u> with other species. Some, though, form a special <u>partnership</u> called a *symbiotic relationship*. Each partner plays a <u>role</u> that is <u>beneficial</u> to the other. For example, when a bee gathers food from a flower, it gets the flower's pollen on it. Then, when it visits another flower of the same kind, it leaves some of the pollen behind. This allows the flower to make seeds.

Write the academic words from the paragraph above next to their correct definitions.

Example: _____*role*_____: the position or job that something or someone has in a particular situation or activity

1. _____: talk to other people and work together with them

2. _____: a relationship in which two or more people, organizations, etc., work together to achieve something

3. _____: good or useful

Use the academic words from the paragraph above to complete the sentences.

4. The two journalists formed a _____ to share information.

5. Donna's _____ at the store is to change the window display every week.

6. Her advice turned out to be very _____.

7. If you work from home instead of at an office, you don't _____ with many people during the day.

Complete the sentences with your own ideas.

Example: Immigrants are beneficial to a neighborhood because of
  the culture they bring .

8. The first person I interact with in the morning is _____.

9. One important role I have in my family is _____.

10. I have a partnership with _____.

WORD STUDY Greek and Latin Roots *para, sitos, virus, nutrire*

Use with textbook page 183.

> **REMEMBER** Knowing Greek or Latin roots can help you understand the meaning of unfamiliar words.
> **Example:** The Latin root *nutrire* means *nourish*. From this root, we get the English word *nutrition*.

Look at the words in the box. Write each word in the chart under its related root.

~~nutrient~~	prepare	dentures	virulent	nutrition	viral
dentist	paralegal	malnutrition	paragraph	antiviral	dental

nutrire ("nourish")	dent ("teeth")	virus ("poison")	para ("beside")
nutrient			

Use your knowledge of the root words to write a definition of each of the following words. Check your work in a dictionary.

1. paralegal _____

2. parasite _____

3. viral _____

4. dentures _____

5. virulent _____

6. malnutrition _____

7. dental _____

8. nutrient _____

READING STRATEGY **CLASSIFY** *Use with textbook page 183.*

REMEMBER When you classify, you arrange words, ideas, objects, texts, or people into groups with common characteristics.

Read the paragraph. Then answer the questions that follow.

My mom laughs when she sees cars pulling up near the house that is three doors down from us. She knows that the drivers are amazed by the Seavers' house. The Seavers love the holidays—all holidays. Whether it's Martin Luther King, Jr. Day, Valentine's Day, Washington's Birthday, Easter, or July 4, the Seavers have their house covered with decorations. On President's Day, they had 100 little flags sticking up in their lawn. On Valentine's Day, every window had cut-out hearts. For Halloween, they covered their yard with fake spiderwebs. Dad frowns disapprovingly, "That looks like too much work." But I agree with my mom. I think the Seavers make all the holidays more fun.

1. List words in this passage that have to do with emotions.

_____

_____

2. List words in this passage that have to do with decorations.

_____

_____

3. List words in this passage that are holidays.

_____

_____

4. List how each member of the writer's family feels about the Seavers.

_____

_____

5. How do you think classifying can make you a better reader?

_____

_____

Choose the best answer for each item. Circle the letter of the correct answer.

1. In exchange for protection by the water buffalo, the oxpecker _____.

   a. feeds on ticks from the buffalo's skin   **b.** feeds on the buffalo's food   **c.** builds its nest in the buffalo's hair

2. The buffalo and the oxpecker have a _____.

   a. mutualistic relationship   **b.** commensal relationship   **c.** parasitic relationship

3. Orchids and trees have a _____.

   a. parasitic relationship   **b.** commensal relationship   **c.** mutualistic relationship

4. In a commensal relationship, one organism is _____.

   a. stronger than the other   **b.** damaged   **c.** neither hurt nor helped

5. In a parasitic relationship, the host is _____.

   a. indifferent   **b.** hurt   **c.** helped

EXTENSION *Use with textbook page 191.*

In this article, you read about mutualistic relationships. Do you have a mutualistic relationship with someone? Write about it on the lines below.

_____

_____

_____

_____

_____

GRAMMAR, USAGE, AND MECHANICS

Compound and Complex Sentences *Use with textbook page 192.*

REMEMBER A compound sentence consists of two independent clauses joined with conjunctions such as *and, but, yet,* or *or.* Each of the two sentences consists of at least a subject and a verb, and expresses a complete thought.
Example: Parents love their children, and children love their parents.
A complex sentence consists of an independent clause and a dependent clause joined with conjunctions such as *after, when, while, since, before,* or *because.* A dependent clause consists of a subject and a verb as well, but it does NOT express a complete thought.
Example: The bush could not survive *because* there were no ants left.
A complex sentence may begin with the dependent or the independent clause. If the complex sentence begins with the dependent clause, use a comma to separate the two.
Example: When two animals are in a symbiotic relationship, they both gain from it.

Read the sentences. Then decide whether each sentence is compound or complex. Write *compound* or *complex* in the space provided.

Example: _*compound*_ : The oxpecker warns the buffalo, and the buffalo feeds the oxpecker.

1. _____ : When the acacia bush releases its sweet liquid, ants flock to feed.

2. _____ : The ants come in droves because the liquid attracts them.

3. _____ : The parasite benefits from the relationship to its host, but the host suffers.

Combine each pair of sentences using the conjunction in parentheses.

Example: (but) Human relationships are supposed to be friendly. Sometimes they are hostile.

Human relationships are supposed to be friendly, but sometimes

they are hostile.

4. (and) I have a cold. My brother has the flu.

_____

5. (after) The mosquito bites its host. The mosquito drinks its host's blood.

_____

WRITING AN EXPOSITORY PARAGRAPH

Write a Classifying Paragraph *Use with textbook page 193.*

This is the three-column chart that Katie completed before writing her paragraph.

Bald eagles	Bottlenose dolphins	Meerkats
Males and females share the duty of sitting on their eggs. One sits while the other looks for food. Eaglets stay with their parents for 8 to 14 weeks.	Male dolphins are not involved in raising their young. Dolphins have a baby about every 3 years. The calf lives with its mother for up to 6 years	Young meerkats are not cared for by their parents. They are cared for by surrounding females. These females protect them from predators.

Complete your own three-column chart classifying something into three categories.

EDIT AND PROOFREAD   *Use with textbook page 200.*

Read the paragraph carefully. Look for mistakes in spelling, punctuation, and grammar. Mark the mistakes with editing marks (textbook page 460). Then rewrite the paragraph correctly on the lines.

> Juan hates it when his mother orders him around. Her latest instruction is simple: She said Son, clean your room." So Juan decided to alfebetize his music collection. He picked up three cds that had falen behind his desk. They were by his favorite singor, Prince. He realized that he had never actually lisened to any of them before. They had fallen behind the desk the day he bought them. Juan decided maybee his mom was right. maybe it wasnt such a bad idea after all to be neet and organized.

_____

_____

_____

_____

_____

_____

_____

_____

_____

_____

_____

Underline the vocabulary items you know and can use well. Review and practice any you haven't underlined. Underline them when you know them well.

Literary Words	Key Words	Academic Words	
foreshadowing	barriers	distributes	authoritative
irony	confrontation	positive	consent
oral tradition	cultivate	rejected	encounter
legend	enemies	residents	reaction
character motive	political	assumed	beneficial
	violence	focus	interact
	commensal	individuals	partnership
	mutualistic	similarities	role
	nature		
	parasites		
	protection		
	symbiosis		

Put a check by the skills you can perform well. Review and practice any you haven't checked off. Check them off when you can perform them well.

Skills	I can . . .
Word Study	☐ spell words using -*s* blends. ☐ recognize and use the suffixes -*er* and -*or*. ☐ recognize and use synonyms. ☐ recognize and use Greek and Latin roots *para, sitos, virus, nutrire*.
Reading Strategies	☐ analyze cultural context. ☐ compare and contrast. ☐ identify with a character. ☐ classify.
Grammar, Usage, and Mechanics	☐ use imperatives. ☐ use independent and dependent clauses. ☐ use expressions to compare and contrast. ☐ use compound and complex sentences.
Writing	☐ write instructions. ☐ write a critique. ☐ write to compare and contrast. ☐ write a classifying paragraph. ☐ write an expository essay.

Name _____ Date _____

Learn about Art with the Smithsonian
American Art Museum *Use with textbook pages 202–203.*

LEARNING TO LOOK

Look at *Placa/Rollcall* by Charles "Chaz" Bojórquez on page 203 in your textbook.
The artist uses shapes in place of letters in this painting. Find the shapes and then
list as many as you can. State facts, not opinions.

Example: _____ *triangle* _____

1. _____   4. _____

2. _____   5. _____

3. _____   6. _____

INTERPRETATION

Look at *Merce C* by Franz Kline on page 202 in your textbook. Imagine that each of
the brushstrokes in the painting is a dancer. Describe his or her movements.

Example: ____*The brushstroke on the right looks like it is moving an arm.*____

_____

_____

_____

_____

_____

_____

What sounds or music is the dancer dancing to? Explain your answer.

_____

_____

Look at *Placa/Rollcall* by Charles "Chaz" Bojórquez again. If you could interview Chaz's friends, whose names appear in his artwork, what would you ask them? Use questions that begin with *Who, Where, When, What, Why,* and *How.*

Example: Where *did you grow up?* _____

7. Who _____

_____

8. Where _____

_____

9. When _____

_____

10. What _____

_____

11. Why _____

_____

12. How _____

_____

Name _____ Date _____

What does home mean?

READING 1: "97 Orchard Street" / "The Pros and Cons of Tenement Life"

VOCABULARY **Key Words** *Use with textbook page 207.*

Write each word in the box next to its definition.

exhibit	inspectors	mission	neighborhood	preserved	tenement

Example: *neighborhood* : a small area of town

1. _____: an assignment or purpose

2. _____: apartment house in a poor area of a city

3. _____: something shown to the public

4. _____: kept from harm or change

5. _____: officials who examine things carefully

Use the words in the box at the top of the page to complete the sentences.

6. The museum's _____ is to tell the story of the old town.

7. We visited an art gallery where a new _____ was on display.

8. The _____ looked around and said the wiring was safe.

9. The residents of the _____ were proud of their new library.

10. The family from China _____ many old Chinese traditions.

Read the paragraph below. Pay attention to the underlined academic words.

Heirlooms are <u>items</u> that are passed down from one family member to another. One <u>benefit</u> of keeping this tradition alive is that heirlooms give children of <u>immigrants</u> a connection to their ancestors' country. The design of the heirloom usually tells something about the <u>cultural</u> background it came from. For example, people in an Irish <u>community</u> sometimes wear a ring called a Claddagh. The ring is usually passed down from parents to their children. The ring shows two hands holding a heart, with a crown on top. These are symbols of ancient Ireland.

Write the letter of the correct definition next to each word.

Example: ___*b*___ cultural

_____ **1.** immigrants

_____ **2.** benefit

_____ **3.** community

_____ **4.** items

a. people who enter another country in order to live there

b. relating to a particular society and its way of life

c. all the people living in one place

d. things in a set, group, or list

e. something that helps you or gives you an advantage

Use the academic words from the exercise above to complete the sentences.

5. The _____ were happy in their adopted country.

6. The annual parade brought together people in the _____.

7. One _____ of a balanced diet is more energy.

8. I inherited several _____ from my grandfather.

Complete the sentences with your own ideas.

Example: Most of the immigrants in my community are from ___*Haiti*___.

9. My most treasured items are _____.

10. One benefit of living in a diverse community is _____.

WORD STUDY   **Silent Letters**   *Use with textbook page 209.*

REMEMBER The letters *gn, bt, mb,* and *kn* stand for one sound, not two. For example: the *g* is silent in *gnome*, the *b* is silent in *indebted*, the *b* is silent in *plumber*, and the *k* is silent in *knead*. Knowing when letters are silent will help you spell and pronounce words correctly.

Read the words in the box below. Then write each word in the correct column in the chart.

designing	knowledge	crumb	gnarled	knack	undoubted
plumber	doubt	doubted	knob	thumb	gnaw

Words with *gn*	Words with *bt*	Words with *mb*	Words with *kn*
designing			

Identify and write the silent letter in each word below.

Example: knoll _____*silent k*_____

1. gnat _____

2. assign _____

3. doubtful _____

4. knot _____

5. tomb _____

6. reign _____

7. knitting _____

8. bomb _____

9. knee _____

Use with textbook page 209.

REMEMBER As you read, try to identify the author's purpose for writing. To do this, read the text carefully. Then ask, "Is the author trying to entertain, to inform, or to persuade me about his or her point of view?"

Read each passage below. Then answer the questions that follow.

1. Dear Principal Rodriguez,

   I am writing to ask you to let high school students take next Friday off. Many other schools in the area are taking the day off because it is a holiday. It is only fair that our high school should have the day off as well. Please consider giving us the day off next Friday.

   Sincerely,
   Jane Smith

   What is Jane Smith's purpose for writing?

   _____

2. What details in the text above helped you to answer question number 1?

   _____

3. Massachusetts is a state in New England. Its neighboring states are Vermont, New York, New Hampshire, Connecticut, and Rhode Island. Massachusetts has a coast along the Atlantic Ocean.

   What is the author's purpose for writing the passage above?

   _____

4. What details in the text above helped you to answer question number 3?

   _____

5. Why is the strategy of identifying the author's purpose important to understanding what you read?

   _____

COMPREHENSION *Use with textbook page 214.*

Choose the best answer for each item. Circle the letter of the correct answer.

1. The museum at 97 Orchard Street in New York City allows visitors to _____.

   a. meet people who grew up at that address
   b. see the immigrant experience firsthand
   c. do the same work that immigrants did in factories

2. The museum shares immigrant history by presenting _____.

   a. audio lectures
   b. apartments of immigrants from long ago
   c. movies and books

3. The nation's most famous gateway for immigrants was at _____.

   a. the Lower East Side
   b. the Upper West Side
   c. Staten Island

4. In the early 1900s, new immigrants found social support and assistance in _____.

   a. their home countries
   b. their jobs
   c. fraternal groups

5. Tenement life created many _____.

   a. cultural problems
   b. health problems
   c. financial problems

EXTENSION *Use with textbook page 215.*

Research five groups of immigrants that came to America. Find out where they settled in large numbers and what neighborhoods they formed there. Write the groups and the names of their new neighborhoods on the chart below.

Immigrant Group	Neighborhoods
Italians	*Little Italy (NYC), North End (Boston)*

GRAMMAR, USAGE, AND MECHANICS

Adjective Clauses with *who* and *which* *Use with textbook page 216.*

REMEMBER An adjective clause describes a noun in a dependent clause. An adjective clause begins with a relative pronoun, such as *who* or *which*. The relative pronoun *who* describes a person or a group of people. The relative pronoun *which* describes one or more things.

Circle the correct relative pronoun in each sentence below.

Example: People ((who)/which) travel are called tourists.

1. People (who / which) arrive in New York City by ship see the Statue of Liberty.

2. The statue, (who / which) is on an island, symbolizes freedom.

3. The man (who / which) designed the statue was French.

4. Visitors explore the city, (who / which) has dozens of neighborhoods.

5. They travel on subway trains, (who / which) run underground.

Circle the correct relative pronoun. Then complete each sentence with your own ideas.

Example: The stories (who/(which)) I enjoy the most ___are mysteries___ .

6. The people (who/which) live in my community _____ .

7. The books (who/which) we read for this class _____ .

8. I have several friends (who/which) _____ .

9. The immigrants (who/which) came to this country a hundred years ago _____

_____ .

10. The homes (who/which) people lived in a hundred years ago _____

_____ .

WRITING AN EXPOSITORY PARAGRAPH

Write a Magazine Article *Use with textbook page 217.*

This is the 5Ws chart that Blaise completed before writing her paragraph.

Who?	*anyone who is curious about the way things work in nature*
What?	*the lightning exhibit*
Where?	*Museum of Science in Boston, Massachusetts*
When?	*whenever the museum is open to visitors*
Why?	*The museum staff members describe how lightning is made, and then they replicate the process right in front of you!*

Complete your own 5Ws chart for a magazine article about an event in your town.

Who?	
What?	
Where?	
When?	
Why?	

What does home mean?

READING 2: "Somebody's Son"

VOCABULARY   **Literary Words** *Use with textbook page 219.*

REMEMBER **Suspense** is a feeling of uncertainty about the outcome of a story. It makes readers wonder what will happen next. Most stories build to a **climax**, or moment of highest intensity. It is often the most suspenseful moment of a story.

Read each situation. Write *yes* if it builds suspense. Write *no* if it does not.

Suspenseful?	Situation
no	Marguerite poured herself a glass of milk and drank it slowly.
1.	Alistair stepped off the plane. The person waiting for him was someone he would never have expected.
2.	The policeman drank his cup of coffee slowly. He loved the taste of hot coffee first thing in the morning.
3.	The door was open just a crack. Through the crack, we could see a figure with a flashlight searching the room. But who could it be?

Write one or two sentences describing each situation. Try to build suspense with your choice of words and details.

Situation	Sentence
a student is running out of time	*The other students were finishing their tests, but Matilda had barely begun the last question. She looked down at the paper and started to panic.*
4. a camper is lost in the woods	
5. two friends enter a foot race	

VOCABULARY **Academic Words** *Use with textbook page 220.*

Read the paragraph below. Pay attention to the underlined academic words.

At our school, the principal's office can <u>correspond</u> with students and their parents through e-mail. We might get a message that our <u>transportation</u> to school will be delayed on a certain day. Or if a snowstorm or some other extreme weather event <u>occurs</u>, a message will <u>indicate</u> that we should not go to school that day.

Write the academic words from the paragraph above next to their correct definitions.

Example: _____*occurs*_____: happens

1. _____: write to someone and receive letters from him or her

2. _____: the process or business of moving people or goods from one place to another

3. _____: say or do something that shows what you want or intend to do

Use the academic words from the paragraph above to complete the sentences.

4. A lunar eclipse, where the moon is in the earth's shadow, _____ twice a year.

5. The bus broke down, so the players needed other _____ to get to the game.

6. Please _____ that you know the answer by raising your hand.

7. I frequently _____ with my grandmother by writing long letters.

Complete the sentences with your own ideas.

Example: If I could, I would correspond with __*Isaac Newton.*_____

8. My favorite mode of transportation is _____

9. Something that occurs every day at my school is _____

10. I often indicate how I feel by _____

REMEMBER Homophones are words that sound the same but are spelled differently and have different meanings. For example, *I, aye,* and *eye* are homophones. *I* means "me"; *aye* means "yes"; and *eye* means "the part of your face that you see with." When you use or read a homophone and are unsure of its meaning and part of speech, look it up in a dictionary.

Write your own definitions for each pair of homophones in the chart. Then check your definitions in a dictionary.

Homophones	Definitions
Example: ad, add	*advertisement, to total*
1. heir, air	
2. bald, bawled	
3. barren, baron	
4. steel, steal	
5. tease, teas	

Write definitions for each pair of homophones below. Use a dictionary if necessary. Then use both words in sentences that show their meanings. You can write a sentence for each word or use both words in one sentence.

Example: tense, tents *nervous; canvas housing structure*

   The kids feel tense when they are camping in tents and see bears coming!

6. bazaar, bizarre _____

_____

7. threw, through _____

_____

8. sighs, size _____

_____

9. leak, leek _____

_____

READING STRATEGY | **SUMMARIZE** *Use with textbook page 221.*

> **REMEMBER** To summarize, find the main ideas and state them in a few short sentences. Leave out details and focus on the most important points.

Read each passage. Then answer the questions that follow.

There are many ways to travel between New York City and Boston. You can take the fast train, which takes 3 ½ hours. You can take the bus, which takes about 4 hours. You can drive in your own car, which takes about 4 hours. You can take a plane, which takes just 1 hour.

1. Summarize the passage above in one sentence.

   _____

2. Which details did you leave out of your summary?

   _____

Homes come in all kinds of shapes and sizes. Igloos are homes made of ice and snow. Log cabins are homes made of wood. Many homes in cities are tall apartment buildings made of steel and concrete. Whatever type of home a person has, all that really matters is that it feels safe and warm.

3. Summarize the passage above in one sentence.

   _____

4. What details did you leave out of your summary?

   _____

5. How can the strategy of summarizing help you to better understand what you read?

   _____

Choose the best answer for each item. Circle the letter of the correct answer.

1. David wrote to his parents to let them know he was _____.

   a. in Baltimore   **b.** hitchhiking home   **c.** going to college

2. To show that it was acceptable for him to come home, he asked that his dad _____.

   a. meet him at the train station   **b.** leave a scarecrow by a tree   **c.** tie a white cloth to a tree

3. Suspense builds in the story every time David _____.

   a. is delayed on his trip   **b.** checks his mail   **c.** falls asleep and nearly misses his stop

4. The story's climax comes when the train passenger _____.

   a. goes to college   **b.** sees the apple tree   **c.** boards the train

5. At the end of the story David finds out that _____.

   a. his father wants to see him   **b.** he isn't welcome at home   **c.** his parents never got the letter

RESPONSE TO LITERATURE *Use with textbook page 229.*

Reread the last line of the story. Then write a short paragraph describing how you think David felt when he heard about the tree.

_____

_____

_____

_____

_____

GRAMMAR, USAGE, AND MECHANICS

Adjectives and Adverbs *Use with textbook page 230.*

> **REMEMBER** An adjective describes a noun. It usually appears before the noun it describes or after a form of the verb *be*. An adverb usually describes a verb or tells how something is done. Many adverbs are formed by adding *-ly* to an adjective. For example, the adjective *quick* becomes the adverb *quickly*. The adjective *careful* becomes the adverb *carefully*.

Read each sentence. Choose the appropriate word to complete the sentence. If the correct word is an adjective, underline it. If the correct word is an adverb, circle it.

Example: The woman standing at the door is very (beautiful/beautifully).

1. An (elegant / elegantly) woman entered the room.

2. The girl (eager / eagerly) awaited her birthday.

3. The party was (wonderful / wonderfully).

4. The angry man spoke (sharp / sharply).

5. The scientist talked about three kinds of (wild / wildly) mushrooms.

Answer each question by writing a sentence with an adjective or an adverb. Use the words in parentheses.

Example: How was the movie? (*be, sad*)

    The movie was sad.

6. What kind of person is he? (*nice, person*)

_____

7. How did she react to the news? (*calmly*)

_____

8. What kind of dancer is she? (*graceful, dancer*)

_____

9. How did he march in the parade? (*proudly*)

_____

10. How is the kitchen? (*be, spotless*)

_____

WRITING AN EXPOSITORY PARAGRAPH

Write a Plot Summary *Use with textbook page 231.*

This is the plot summary chart that Andrew completed before writing his paragraph.

Characters *David, his father and mother, strangers, a passenger*	
Setting *journey away from and back to David's home in Maryland*	
Conflict *David ran away from home and wants to return.*	
Main events *David runs away but wants to return. He writes a letter asking his parents to tie a white cloth to a tree if he can come back.*	
Resolution *He goes home and there are pieces of cloth tied to almost every one of the tree's branches!*	

Complete your own plot summary chart for a story from a book, film, or television show you know well.

Characters
Setting
Conflict
Main events
Resolution

UNIT 4

What does home mean?

READING 3: "Operation Migration"

VOCABULARY **Key Words** *Use with textbook page 233.*

Write each word in the box next to its definition.

| endangered species | migration | monitor | population | rare | refuge |

Example: _migration_ : the movement of animals from one region to another

1. _____ : the number of animals or people living in an area

2. _____ : not seen or found very often

3. _____ : carefully watch for changes

4. _____ : a safe place set aside for people or animals

5. _____ : a kind of animal whose numbers are so small it risks becoming extinct

Use the words in the box at the top of the page to complete the sentences.

6. Most of the _____ of that species is found in Asia.

7. That bird is an _____, and there are not many left.

8. The scientists will _____ that group of baboons for six months.

9. The monarch butterfly _____ is a beautiful sight.

10. The bald eagle was once a very _____ bird.

Read the paragraph below. Pay attention to the underlined academic words.

> Last week we had a <u>substitute</u> teacher. She asked us to get into groups and discuss the meaning of the last reading assignment. She walked around to listen as we discussed. She took an unusual <u>route</u> through the classroom, so we didn't know which group she would visit next. After we finished, she asked us to write a paragraph about the <u>outcome</u> of our discussions. The earlier <u>interaction</u> with my group helped me write my paragraph.

Write the letter of the correct definition next to each word.

Example: ___c___ outcome

_____ 1. substitute

_____ 2. route

_____ 3. interaction

a. the activity of talking with other people and working together with them

b. someone who does someone else's job

c. the final result of a meeting, process, etc.

d. the way from one place to another

Use the academic words from the exercise above to complete the sentences.

4. The teacher took notes on the _____ between the two children.

5. Migrating reindeer use the same _____ every year in search of food.

6. The process was different whenever we worked together, but the

   _____ was always the same.

7. When our teacher was sick, a _____ taught our class for the day.

Complete the sentences with your own ideas.

Example: The easiest route to the ocean is ___*along the river.*___

8. My interaction with the principal is always _____

9. My favorite substitute teacher is _____

10. You can change the outcome of a situation by _____

Name _____ Date _____

REMEMBER A suffix is a letter or group of letters added to the end of a base word to make a new word. Adding suffixes to base words usually changes the word's part of speech and meaning. The suffix *-ion*, for example, means "an act or process" and makes a verb into a noun. For nouns that end in silent *e*, drop the *e* before adding *-ion*, as in *elevate* and *elevation*.

Look at the chart below. Add the suffix *-ion* to create a new word. Write the new word on the chart. Then write the meaning of the new word. Notice how the part of speech of the word changes when you add *-ion*.

Base Word (verb)	Suffix	New Word (noun)	Definition
educate	-ion	*education*	*schooling*
1. adopt	-ion		
2. motivate	-ion		
3. attract	-ion		
4. eliminate	-ion		
5. depress	-ion		

Create a noun by adding the suffix *-ion* to each verb below. Then write a sentence with the noun.

Verb	Noun	Sentence
Example: inform	*information*	*I need some information about sandhill cranes.*
6. delete		
7. confuse		
8. correct		
9. protect		
10. translate		

Use with textbook page 235.

> **REMEMBER** You can monitor comprehension by rereading a text. Make a list of difficult words. Try to figure out their meanings from the context, or look them up in a dictionary. Then restate the information in your own words.

Read each passage. Then answer the questions and follow directions.

Every Christmas, I visit my grandparents in Maine. We have stayed with them for Christmas every year since I was a little girl. We pack up the family car with presents and suitcases. Then we drive hundreds and hundreds of miles from our home in Virginia to Maine. The trip begins early in the morning and we reach my grandparents' house in time for dinner. When we get there, my grandparents have their Christmas tree decorated with lights. We sing carols and put our presents under the tree. The countryside is almost always covered with beautiful, white snow. I love Christmas in Maine.

1. Are there any difficult words in the passage? If so, write them down. Try to figure out their meanings from the context, or look them up in a dictionary.

_____

2. What is the passage about?

_____

I feel very strongly that high school students should have less homework. Most of us work an after-school job every day to earn pocket money. By the time we get home and have dinner, we're exhausted. We just want to relax, watch some TV, talk with our friends, and go to bed. We do not have the energy to take out our school books and spend an hour or two on homework.

3. Are there any difficult words in the passage? If so, write them down. Try to figure out their meanings from the context, or look them up in a dictionary.

_____

4. What is the passage about?

_____

_____

5. How can the strategy of monitoring comprehension help you become a better reader?

_____

COMPREHENSION   *Use with textbook page 240.*

Choose the best answer for each item. Circle the letter of the correct answer.

1. The whooping cranes became endagered because of the _____.

   a. whooping crane   **b.** expansion of American   **c.** explosion in the
        disease   cities   domestic cat population

2. The goal of Operation Migration is to _____.

   a. produce a second   **b.** raise awareness of   **c.** train birds to
        migratory flock   endangered species   trust humans

3. Sandhill cranes were used to test Operation Migration because there are _____.

   a. only a few of them   **b.** many of them   **c.** people who like them

4. The flight of the sandhill cranes behind the ultralight took _____.

   a. as long as cranes   **b.** much longer than   **c.** much less time than
        flying alone   cranes flying alone   cranes flying alone

5. Whooping cranes are still in danger because _____.

   a. humans hunt them   **b.** there are only 15 left   **c.** all whooping cranes
        for sport   in the world   are part of one
                                                                         single flock

EXTENSION   *Use with textbook page 241.*

Research five endangered species. On the table below, write the remaining population for each species and where it is found. Then mark each animal's territory on a map.

Species	Population	Habitat
Hawaiian duck	2,200	Hawaii

Subject-Verb Agreement *Use with textbook page 242.*

REMEMBER In every sentence, the verb must agree with the subject of the sentence.
If the subject of the sentence is singular, the verb must be singular.
Examples: The bird nests. He touches the ground.
If the subject is plural, the verb must be plural.
Examples: The birds nest. They touch the ground.
Note: When the subject is plural or when the pronoun *I, we, you,* or *they* is the subject, do not add *-s* or *-es* to a verb in the simple present.

Circle the correct verb in each sentence below.

Example: Most students (finish / finishes) their homework carefully.

1. The bird (catch / catches) a fish.

2. We (protect / protects) the cranes.

3. Cranes (need / needs) wetlands.

4. It (happen / happens) gradually.

5. You (reach / reaches) the end of your journey.

Circle the correct verb. Then complete each sentence based on "Operation Migration."

Example: I (help / helps) others _by volunteering_____.

6. The birds (migrate / migrates) _____.

7. International law (protect / protects) _____.

8. The wind (help / helps) _____.

9. The pilots (wear / wears) _____.

10. Naturalists (watch / watches) _____.

WRITING AN EXPOSITORY PARAGRAPH

Write a Problem-and-Solution Paragraph *Use with textbook page 243.*

This is the problem-and-solution chart that Pablo completed before writing his paragraph.

> **Problem**
> The whooping crane is threatened with extinction.

> **Solution**
> 1. Put the bird on the endangered species list and protect its breeding grounds.
>
> 2. Create a second migratory flock by training chicks to follow a new migration route.

Complete your own problem-and-solution chart for a paragraph you write to describe a problem in your school and how it was solved.

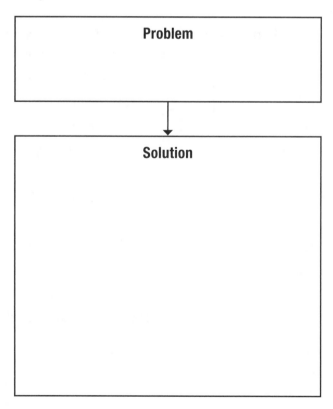

> **Problem**

> **Solution**

What does home mean?

READING 4: From *The Lotus Seed*

VOCABULARY **Literary Words** *Use with textbook page 245.*

REMEMBER The **speaker** of a poem is the character who tells the poem. A **symbol** is anything that stands for something else. It has its own meaning, but can also stand for an idea or feeling.

Read each sentence. Write whether it contains a symbol or a line of a poem narrated by a speaker.

Sense	Description
speaker	*I think you're like a summer day, / Please listen and I'll count the ways*
1.	We stand watching / leaves falling in autumn
2.	The statue represented happiness.
3.	Do you remember the smell of evening? / We shared it, smiling

Read the two poems below. Circle the clues that help you determine who the speaker is. Then write who the speaker is. The first clue has been circled.

When I was ten-and-three
I'm certain I did see
A tiny brontosaurus
I'm sure it said to me
"I live beneath a certain tree
Right here, deep in the forest"
Dear grandson, this is true!
It might happen to you . . .

4. _____

We float above waiting,
Rumble and light,
High overhead.
Gather and burst
Then tumble and down,
Splatter and splash
We pool at your feet
And race down your rivers
And dampen your hair.
How else would we meet?

5. _____

VOCABULARY **Academic Words** *Use with textbook page 246.*

Read the paragraph below. Pay attention to the underlined academic words.

My grandmother <u>removed</u> the ruby ring she was wearing and showed it to me. She said, "I'm very <u>attached</u> to this ring. My own grandmother gave it to me." I looked closely at the small, but very beautiful ring. By my grandmother's smile, I could see that the ring was a <u>source</u> of great pleasure for her. "A ruby can <u>symbolize</u> love," she said.

Write the academic words from the paragraph above next to their correct definitions.

Example: _____*source*_____: where something comes from

1. _____: represent a quality or feeling

2. _____: emotionally connected to

3. _____: took something away from where it was

Use the academic words from the paragraph above to complete the sentences.

4. On the American flag, the stars _____ the 50 states.

5. The thief _____ the jewel from the glass case.

6. The puppies were _____ to their mother right away.

7. The _____ of the quotation is from a book that I read years ago.

Complete the sentences with your own ideas.

Example: Children grow very attached to ___*their pets*_____.

8. Doves often symbolize _____.

9. The source of my motivation is _____.

10. When I get home, I usually remove _____.

REMEMBER The long *o* sound can be spelled several different ways. These include *o* as in *cold*, *oa* as in *roast*, *o_e* as in *bone*, and *ow* as in *show*. Knowing these sound-spelling relationships will help you spell and say words with long *o* correctly.

Read the words in the box below. Then write each word in the correct column in the chart.

~~pagoda~~	moan	swallow	zone	toast	snow
aglow	loaf	hello	vote	ago	telephone

Words with long o spelled *o*	Words with long o spelled *oa*	Words with long o spelled *o_e*	Words with long o spelled *ow*
pagoda			

For each word below, write the letter or letters that stand for the long *o* sound.

Example: colt _____long o spelled o_____

1. boast _____

2. hold _____

3. strove _____

4. row _____

5. float _____

6. unknown _____

7. grown _____

8. nowhere _____

9. tone _____

READING STRATEGY | ANALYZE TEXT STRUCTURE

Use with textbook page 247.

REMEMBER When you read, analyze text structure by studying the way the parts of a text are arranged. Remember that poems and plays have a special text structure. They are arranged in lines and groups of lines called stanzas. Narrative poems are written in verse. Punctuation doesn't always follow the same rules in poetry as it does in other types of text.

Read each passage below. Then answer the questions that follow each passage.

> Every day
> In every way
> I try to grow
> Strong and proud

1. What is the text structure of the passage above?

   _____

2. Are there rhyming lines in the passage above? If so, what are they?

   _____

> KIM: We have to solve the mystery!
> JUAN: I told you already. It's too dangerous!
> KIM: If we don't solve it, who will?
> JUAN: Promise me that one day, you'll stop dragging me into your adventures!
> KIM: Does that mean you'll help me solve the mystery?
> JUAN: I guess I have no choice.

3. What is the text structure of the passage above?

   _____

4. What do the words in bold represent in this text structure?

   _____

5. How can the strategy of analyzing text structure help you become a better reader?

   _____

Choose the best answer for each item. Circle the letter of the correct answer.

1. The speaker's grandmother takes the lotus seed in order to _____.

   a. give it to her grandchildren

   b. remember the emperor

   c. remember Vietnam

2. When the grandmother's family left the country, she _____.

   a. took the lotus seed

   b. took her hair combs

   c. took water from the River of Perfume

3. For the grandmother, the lotus seed symbolizes _____.

   a. a new life in the United States

   b. the old ways in Vietnam

   c. the Vietnam War

4. When Bà sees the lotus blossom growing in her garden, she feels _____.

   a. remorse

   b. anger

   c. hope

5. The seed allows the speaker to _____.

   a. connect her life to her grandmother's life in Vietnam

   b. plant her own garden

   c. see the golden dragon throne of the emperor

RESPONSE TO LITERATURE *Use with textbook page 253.*

In *The Lotus Seed*, the seed acts as a symbol for the grandmother. Think of your own family and your heritage. What symbol would you choose to represent your memories and traditions? Write a short paragraph describing this symbol.

_____

_____

_____

_____

_____

GRAMMAR, USAGE, AND MECHANICS

Adverb Clauses of Time *Use with textbook page 254.*

REMEMBER Adverb clauses of time express *when*. The adverbs *when* and *whenever* have different meanings. *When* refers to an event that happened once. *Whenever* refers to an event that happened many times. An adverb clause is a dependent clause. It may be placed before or after the main clause in a sentence. When an adverb clause comes at the beginning of a sentence, it is followed by a comma.

Underline the adverb clause in each sentence below.

Example: Dinners taste especially good <u>when my mother cooks</u>.

1. Whenever my aunt visits, we have fun.

2. I plan to be a doctor when I am older.

3. When you know the answer, raise your hand.

4. The mother smiled whenever she saw her children.

5. The caterpillar will turn into a butterfly when it matures.

Write sentences with the correct adverb clauses in parentheses.

Example: (when / whenever autumn arrives)

   When autumn arrived this year, the leaves turned yellow and red.

6. (when / whenever I grow up)

   _____

7. (when / whenever they go to school)

   _____

8. (when / whenever I reread my favorite book)

   _____

9. (when / whenever the mail comes today)

   _____

10. (when / whenever it rains)

   _____

Write a Response to Literature *Use with textbook page 255.*

This is the idea web that Madeline completed before writing her paragraph.

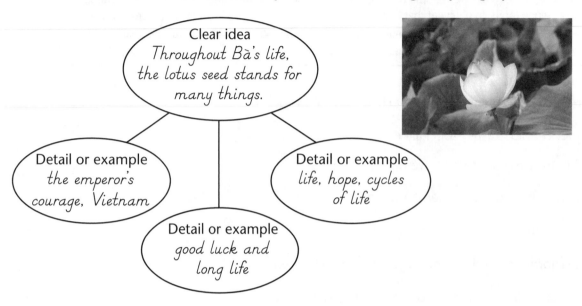

Complete your own idea web for a response to a story or another piece of literature.

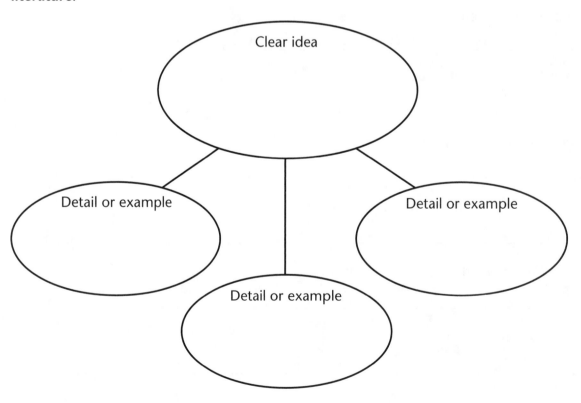

EDIT AND PROOFREAD   *Use with textbook page 262.*

Read the paragraph below carefully. Look for mistakes in spelling, punctuation, and grammar. Mark the mistakes with editing marks (textbook page 460). Then rewrite the paragraph correctly on the lines below.

During the summer, several students from the local high school had a fun volunteer expereince. The New Hope Clinic, who provides free medical consultation to neighborhood families, is located near the school. One of the students' tasks was to help make patients feel at home The students would offers refreshments to the Patients and engage them in conversation to make them comfortable. When pateints couldn't read or write, the students would assist them. Each student also spent a day shadowing one of the nurses, which were happy to provide guidance. The nurses prepare the patients for docter visits, take down patient informatoin, and provide first aid to patients that need it. One of our students, Enrique Martin, stayed for an extra week at the end of the summer. He followed Dr. dalek around the office, watching him treat patients. Enrique has decided to study medicine next year at college

Underline the vocabulary items you know and can use well. Review and practice any you haven't underlined. Underline them when you know them well.

Literary Words	Key Words	Academic Words	
suspense	exhibit	benefit	interaction
climax	inspectors	community	outcome
speaker	mission	cultural	route
symbol	neighborhood	immigrants	substitute
	preserved	items	attached
	tenement	correspond	removed
	endangered species	indicate	source
	migration	occurs	symbolize
	monitor	transportation	
	population		
	rare		
	refuge		

Put a check by the skills you can perform well. Review and practice any you haven't checked off. Check them off when you can perform them well.

Skills	I can . . .
Word Study	☐ spell words with silent letters. ☐ recognize and use homophones. ☐ recognize and use the suffix -*ion*. ☐ recognize and spell words with long *o*.
Reading Strategies	☐ identify author's purpose. ☐ summarize. ☐ monitor comprehension. ☐ analyze text structure.
Grammar, Usage, and Mechanics	☐ use adjective clauses with *who* and *which*. ☐ use adjectives and adverbs correctly. ☐ use subject-verb agreement. ☐ use adverb clauses of time.
Writing	☐ write a magazine article. ☐ write a plot summary. ☐ write a problem-and-solution paragraph. ☐ write a response to a piece of literature. ☐ write an expository essay.

Learn about Art with the Smithsonian
American Art Museum *Use with textbook pages 264–265.*

LEARNING TO LOOK

Look at *Camas para Sueños* by Carmen Lomas Garza on page 264 in your textbook.
Use that artwork to complete the web diagram below. For each "string" in the
diagram, write a detail that you see. State facts, not opinions.

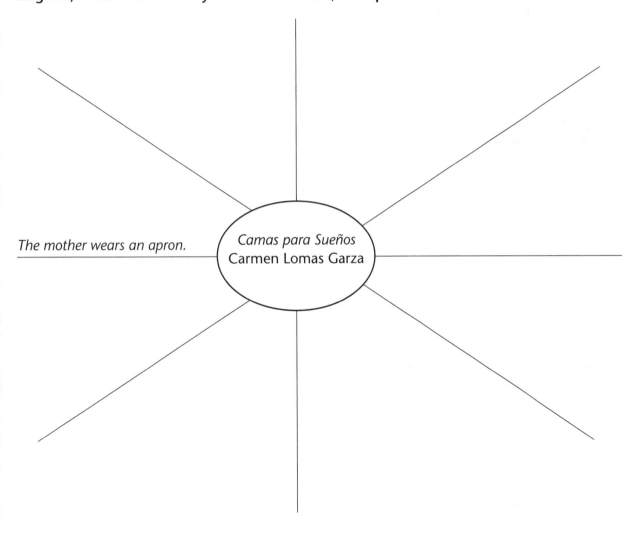

The mother wears an apron.

Camas para Sueños
Carmen Lomas Garza

INTERPRETATION

Look at *The Ocean Is the Dragon's World* by Hung Liu on page 265 in your textbook. What title would you give Hung Liu's painting?

Example: _I would call this painting The Great Empress because it shows a_
royal Chinese woman.

Write your title and explain why you chose it.

_____

_____

COMPARE & CONTRAST

Look at *The Ocean Is the Dragon's World* and *Camas para Sueños* again. Write three details about the woman in *The Ocean Is the Dragon's World*.

Example: _The woman has very long fingernails._

1. _____

2. _____

3. _____

Write three details about the mother in *Camas para Sueños*.

4. _____

5. _____

6. _____

How are the two figures similar?

_____

_____

How are the two figures different?

_____

_____

What is the human spirit?

UNIT 5

READING 1: From *César Chávez: We Can Do It!*

VOCABULARY **Key Words** *Use with textbook page 269.*

Write each word in the box next to its definition.

chemicals	crops	discrimination	migrant workers	strike	union

Example: ___*chemicals*___ : solids, liquids, or gases used in chemistry

1. _____ : people who go to another area or country to find work

2. _____ : stop working because of a disagreement about pay or working conditions

3. _____ : plants such as corn or wheat that farmers sell

4. _____ : an organization of workers that bargains as a group

5. _____ : treating one group of people differently from another in an unfair way

Use the words in the box at the top of the page to complete the sentences.

6. Members of the _____ asked for more pay.

7. The workers decided to protest by going on _____.

8. The fields have produced more _____ this summer.

9. _____ move to wherever they can find jobs.

10. Because Sheila was not treated the same as the men in her office, she accused her boss of _____.

Read the paragraph below. Pay attention to the underlined academic words.

A trade union is a group of workers who bargain together to improve their wages, benefits and working conditions. The idea behind a union is that workers who stand together have a stronger <u>impact</u>. One of the best-known unions is The American Federation of Labor. It was <u>founded</u> in 1886 by Samuel Gompers. Its first aim was to protect the safety of workers who performed manual <u>labor</u>. Gompers' <u>persistence</u> led to better pay, shorter hours and more job security for all union members.

Write the letter of the correct definition next to each word.

Example: __c__ founded

_____ 1. labor

_____ 2. persistence

_____ 3. impact

a. work that requires a lot of physical effort

b. determination to do something even though it is difficult or other people oppose it

c. established a business, organization, school, etc.

d. effect that an event or situation has on someone or something

Use the academic words from the exercise above to complete the sentences.

4. The school was _____ in 1861, but moved in 1916.

5. The speech had a great _____ on everyone who heard it.

6. Construction workers have a job that requires a lot of hard _____.

7. He didn't know the answer right away, but with his _____, he finally got it.

Complete the sentences with your own ideas.

Example: Students who show great persistence _*often do well in school*_.

8. The last experience that had a great impact on me was

_____.

9. Our town was founded in _____.

10. The last time I did hard labor was _____.

WORD STUDY **Capitalization** *Use with textbook page 271.*

> **REMEMBER** Capitalize the word *I*, the first letter of the first word in a sentence, all proper nouns, names, and titles of people. Also capitalize geographical terms (and streets, cities, states, countries, continents), historical events (eras, calendar items), and the names of ethnic groups, national groups, and languages.

Look at the chart below. Capitalize each word correctly. Write the correct word in the chart. Then write the rule.

Incorrect Capitalization	Correct Capitalization	Rule
Today i walk the dog.	*I*	*Capitalize I.*
1. the moon is full tonight.		
2. My father is dr. lee.		
3. We visit the grand canyon.		
4. Tomorrow is thanksgiving.		
5. Risa studies spanish.		

Look at the sentences below. Write corrected sentences on the lines.

Example: a new chinese restaurant opened on main street.

> *A new Chinese restaurant opened on Main Street.*

6. the red cross, a health group, went to haiti where many people speak french.

_____

7. we study the renaissance and the revolutionary war in mr. smith's class.

_____

8. i live at 22 vine avenue in st. louis, missouri.

_____

9. the empire state building and the statue of liberty are located in new york city.

_____

10. my birthday is on the last monday in may, the same as memorial day.

_____

Use with textbook page 271.

> **REMEMBER** When you read, distinguish fact from opinion. A fact is a statement that can be proven, and it can be checked with research. An opinion is a person's point of view about a topic. Writers often state opinions with adjectives and with such words as *I think, I believe, I suppose,* and *personally.*

Read each paragraph. Then answer the questions below.

1. Some boys go to all boy schools. I think those schools are a great idea.

   Which statement above is a fact?

   _____

2. Which statement in #1 is an opinion?

   _____

3. Some dogs weigh only a few pounds, but others are huge. Tiny dogs are the cutest.

   Which statement above is a fact?

   _____

4. Which statement in #3 is an opinion?

   _____

5. How can the strategy of distinguishing fact from opinion help you become a better reader?

   _____

   _____

Name _____ Date _____

Choose the best answer for each item. Circle the letter of the correct answer.

1. César Chávez's family became farm workers _____.

   a. during the Depression   **b.** during the
   Roaring Twenties   **c.** when Chávez founded
   the NFWA

2. César Chávez saw that _____.

   a. migrant workers received
   good wages   **b.** migrant workers were
   treated unfairly   **c.** a migrant workers had
   good benefits

3. César started the NFWA to _____.

   a. give farm workers a union   **b.** get more publicity   **c.** rejoin the U.S. Navy

4. The 1965 boycott against California grape growers _____.

   a. was successful   **b.** ended in failure   **c.** went unnoticed

5. César's work on behalf of farmers resulted in _____.

   a. further crackdowns   **b.** new laws protecting
   workers' rights   **c.** a sharp increase in the
   prices of California
   grapes

EXTENSION   *Use with textbook page 279.*

César Chávez tried to help migrant workers, whose lives were difficult. Think about farm labor and about moving around a lot. Write a paragraph about why it would be difficult to be a migrant worker.

_____

_____

_____

_____

_____

GRAMMAR, USAGE, AND MECHANICS

Inseparable Phrasal Verbs *Use with textbook page 280.*

REMEMBER A phrasal verb is made up of a verb and one or more prepositions. The meaning of a phrasal verb differs from the meaning of the original verb.
Example: *Work* means *to labor*, but the phrasal verb *work out* means *to exercise*.
When a phrasal verb is inseparable, a noun or pronoun cannot be placed between the verb and the preposition that follows it.
Example: She dropped out of the race.
Notice that *the race* must follow the phrasal verb *dropped out of*.

Underline the phrasal verb in each sentence below.

Example: My mother <u>works out</u> every day.

1. He got into the backseat of the car.

2. She was not feeling well, and yesterday she came down with a cold.

3. When you are walking, hold on to the handrail so that you do not fall.

Read the definitions of each phrasal verb in parentheses. Then write a sentence with the phrasal verb. (Some phrasal verbs have more than one meaning. Use the meaning that is given here.)

Example: (wait up for = stay awake until someone arrives)

Whenever I go out in the evening, my mother waits up for me.

4. (look after = take care of someone)

_____

5. (come across = find something accidentally or unexpectedly)

_____

WRITING A PERSUASIVE PARAGRAPH

Write an Advertisement *Use with textbook page 281.*

This is the word web that Andrew completed before writing his paragraph.

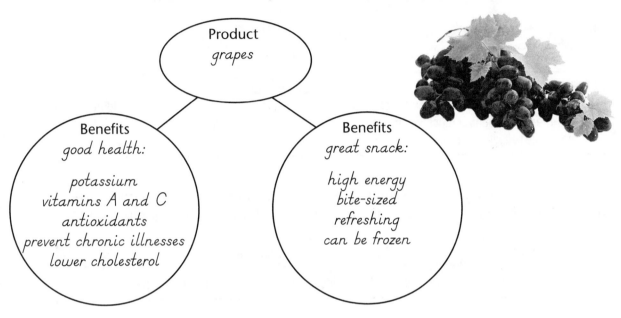

Product
grapes

Benefits
good health:

potassium
vitamins A and C
antioxidants
prevent chronic illnesses
lower cholesterol

Benefits
great snack:

high energy
bite-sized
refreshing
can be frozen

Complete your own word web, and use it to write an advertisement for a product of your choice.

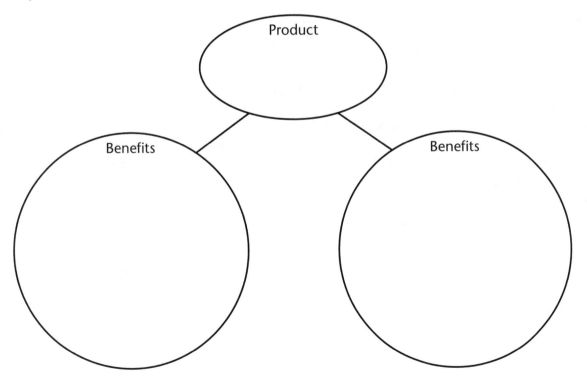

Product

Benefits

Benefits

What is the human spirit?

READING 2: "The Scholarship Jacket"

VOCABULARY   **Literary Words** *Use with textbook page 283.*

REMEMBER A **dialogue** is a conversation between characters. Dialogue is shown with quotation marks. Quotation marks let you know which character is speaking and how the dialogue should be read. The **theme** is a central message in a story. Usually it is not stated directly. You must decide what the theme is by looking closely at the work.

Read each sentence below. If a sentence contains dialogue, write *yes* in the space provided. If a sentence does not contain dialogue, write *no* in the space provided.

Dialogue?	Sentence
yes	Darrell said, "You should come to dinner with Jen and me."
1.	"I've been listening to this song all day," she said, grinning.
2.	We told them we would show up later in the evening.
3.	It's always been easy for her.
4.	I responded, "I don't think it exists."

Read the dialogue below. Answer the question below.

"How are you doing?" Sarah asked, sitting beside Leah.
"Not great!" Leah replied. "I haven't finished my work and it's so late." She sighed.
Sarah smiled helpfully. "Would you like me to stay up a while with you?" she asked.
Leah beamed back. "Thanks, I really could use some help."
"Excellent!" Sarah said. "I'll make cocoa."

5. What is one theme of the passage above? _____

Name _____ Date _____

VOCABULARY Academic Words *Use with textbook page 284.*

Read the paragraph below. Pay attention to the underlined academic words.

Our school principal was a member of Hasty Pudding Theatricals. This group is made up of Harvard University students and is the oldest academic theater group in the United States. The name comes from an early policy where members had to bring a pot of hasty pudding to gatherings. One famous Hasty Pudding tradition is that men perform all the roles, both male and female. Women, like our principal, don't perform, but they can direct and work backstage.

Write the academic words from the paragraph above next to their correct definitions.

Example: _____*policy*_____: a plan that is agreed to by a political party, government, or organization

1. _____: someone who is in charge of a school

2. _____: a belief or custom that has existed for a long time

3. _____: relating to work done in schools, colleges, or universities

Use the academic words from the exercise above to complete the sentences.

4. Each new student in our school has a chance to meet the _____.

5. The company changed its _____ to allow longer vacations.

6. The student enjoyed both athletic and _____ success.

7. In some families, it's a _____ to pray before each meal.

Complete the sentences with your own ideas.

Example: The principal of my school is named _*Mr. Ward*_.

8. The academic subject that I find most challenging is

_____.

9. I find the tradition of _____ interesting.

10. I believe that the government can make things better for citizens by changing its _____ policy.

Use with textbook page 285.

> **REMEMBER** In English, many words end with a consonant and *-le* as in *thimble*, *-al* as in *mental*, or *-el* as in *gavel*. There are no rules for spelling these words, so it's best to memorize the spelling for each.

Read the words in the box below. Then write each word in the correct column in the chart.

~~tickle~~	lapel	rental	sample	
corral	dispel	hotel	example	oriental

Consonant + *-le*	Consonant + *-al*	Consonant + *-el*
tickle		

Underline the two-word letter pattern at the end of each word below. Then write a sentence using the word. Use a dictionary if needed.

Example: divisib<u>le</u>   *Four, six, and eight are divisible by two.*

1. pickle   _____

2. canal   _____

3. capital   _____

4. novel   _____

5. sentimental   _____

6. camel   _____

7. candle   _____

READING STRATEGY | **MAKE INFERENCES** *Use with textbook page 285.*

> **REMEMBER** Making inferences helps you figure out information that an author does not give directly. As you read, think about the characters and the setting, as well as your own experiences.

Read each paragraph and answer the questions that follow.

When Libby's dad signed her up for the swim club she was angry. The first day, she could swim only two laps, while kids half her age swam for hours without getting tired. But after the first month, she could swim twenty laps without stopping. When Libby told her dad that the coach wanted her to join a swim meet, he was surprised by her reaction.

1. What can you infer about Libby's reaction from the passage above?

_____

_____

2. What event from your own experience has helped you understand Libby's feelings?

_____

_____

Dan and Evan had been best friends since second grade, even though they were complete opposites. Dan loved sports. He played baseball, soccer, lacrosse, and football. Evan dreamed of being a famous movie director. Then Carlos moved into the house between the two boys. Carlos loved movies just as much as Evan did.

3. What can you infer about how Carlos' arrival may affect the friendship between Dan and Evan?

_____

_____

4. What event or knowledge from your own experience helped you to make an inference about the passage?

_____

_____

5. How do you think making inferences can help you to understand what you read better?

_____

_____

_____

Choose the best answer for each item. Circle the letter of the correct answer.

1. Each year in Marta's school a scholarship jacket was awarded to _____.

   a. the best athlete in the school

   b. the student who had the highest grades for eight years

   c. the child of a school board member

2. The board was going to give the jacket to Joann because _____.

   a. she had the highest grades

   b. Marta didn't want it

   c. her father was important in the town

3. The board changed its policy about the jacket being free to _____.

   a. have a reason to award it to Joann

   b. raise some extra money

   c. help Marta understand what it was worth

4. Marta's grandfather refused to pay for the jacket because _____.

   a. Marta had earned it

   b. it was too expensive

   c. he was busy with his work

5. In the end the principal decided to _____.

   a. ignore the whole situation

   b. award the jacket to Joann because she could pay for it

   c. do the right thing and award it to Marta

RESPONSE TO LITERATURE *Use with textbook page 295.*

Imagine the graduation ceremony that takes place after the events in "The Scholarship Jacket." Is Grandfather there? Are the teachers there? How is Marta dressed? How does she feel? Draw a picture of the scene in the space below.

GRAMMAR, USAGE, AND MECHANICS

Punctuation in Quotations *Use with textbook page 296.*

> **REMEMBER** Place quotation marks (" ") around quoted speech (what someone says) and capitalize the first word of quoted speech. Use a comma to separate quoted speech from the phrase that identifies the speaker.
> **Example:** She said, "You did a good job."
> When the quoted speech ends with a question mark (**?**) or an exclamation point (**!**), use that mark instead of the comma.
> **Example:** "What a great job you did!" she exclaimed.
> When the phrase that identifies the speaker comes in the middle of quoted speech, use one comma after the first part of the speech and another comma after the phrase.
> **Example:** "You did a good job," she said, "and I'm proud of you."

Put a ✓ next to the sentence in each pair that is correctly punctuated.

_____ 1. The teacher said, "You have made good progress."

_____   The teacher said, You have made good progress.

_____ 2. "Run with the ball" the coach exclaimed.

_____   "Run with the ball!" the coach exclaimed.

_____ 3. "Who won the scholarship," asked the principal.

_____   "Who won the scholarship?" asked the principal.

_____ 4. "Write your name on every page" said the teacher.

_____   "Write your name on every page," said the teacher.

_____ 5. "Study hard," she said, "and you will surely do well."

_____   "Study hard," she said, and you will surely do well."

Fix each of the sentences below by adding correct punctuation.

6. My name is Maria she said

7. He said Tomorrow is my birthday

8. What is your name she asked

9. What a good idea he exclaimed

10. I'm having a party she said and I'd like you to come

Write a Review *Use with textbook page 297.*

This is the idea web that Blaise completed before writing her paragraph.

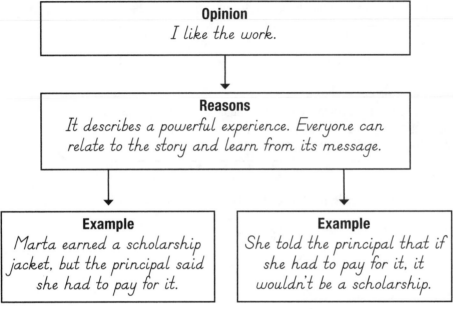

Opinion
I like the work.

↓

Reasons
It describes a powerful experience. Everyone can relate to the story and learn from its message.

Example
Marta earned a scholarship jacket, but the principal said she had to pay for it.

Example
She told the principal that if she had to pay for it, it wouldn't be a scholarship.

Complete your own idea web for a review of a book, CD, play, or film.

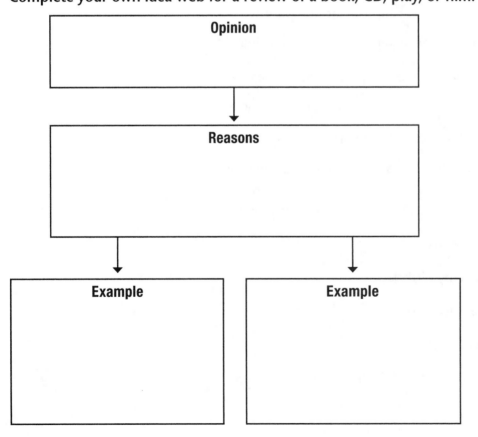

Opinion

↓

Reasons

Example

Example

Name _____ Date _____

What is the human spirit?

READING 3: "Listen Up"

VOCABULARY **Key Words** *Use with textbook page 299.*

Write each word in the box next to its definition.

| accomplish | communicate | hearing impaired | obstacle | opponent | sign language |

Example: _____*obstacle*_____: something that makes it difficult for you to succeed

1. _____: succeed in doing something

2. _____: a language for the deaf, using hand movements instead of
spoken words

3. _____: exchange information or conversation with other people

4. _____: someone who tries to defeat another person or team in
a competition

5. _____: unable to hear well or at all

Use the words in the box at the top of the page to complete the sentences.

6. The deaf woman was able to converse using _____.

7. The young tennis player was nervous about meeting his _____.

8. Will you be able to _____ your goal this week?

9. Some good friends can _____ without saying a word.

10. The biggest _____ to living in Antarctica is staying warm.

Read the paragraph below. Pay attention to the underlined academic words.

> Brainstorming is when a <u>team</u> of people work together to come up with ideas and solve problems. <u>Prior</u> to the 1930s, there was no name for this method. Then advertising executive Alex Faickney Osborn coined the phrase "brainstorming." He could <u>perceive</u> brainstorming to be a very effective problem-solving technique. He felt that the more workers he got to <u>participate</u> in a brainstorming session, the quicker a problem would be solved.

Write the letter of the correct definition next to each word.

Example: __c__ perceive   **a.** before

_____ **1.** team   **b.** take part in an activity or event

_____ **2.** prior   **c.** understand or think about something in a particular way

_____ **3.** participate   **d.** a group of people who compete against another group in a sport, game, etc.

Use the academic words from the exercise above to complete the sentences.

4. The coach recruited five new players for her _____.

5. Mayor Burrell invited every citizen to _____ in the festival.

6. Three people can _____ the same event in three different ways.

7. _____ to 1973, my family lived in Arizona.

Complete the sentences with your own ideas.

Example: ___*My grandfather*___ has told me many stories about prior generations.

8. A team I would like to join is _____.

9. I like to participate in _____.

10. It's sometimes difficult to perceive the problems of _____.

Name _____ Date _____

REMEMBER Antonyms are words that have opposite or nearly opposite meanings. For example, *near* is an antonym for *far.* Learning antonyms helps you express your exact meaning and figure out the meaning of words you do not know.

Look at the chart below. Write an antonym for each word. Use a thesaurus or a dictionary if needed.

Words	Antonym
ending	*beginning*
1. friend	
2. distant	
3. optimistic	
4. defeat	
5. agitated	

Look at the chart below. Write an antonym for each word. Then write a sentence using the antonym. Use a thesaurus or a dictionary if needed.

Word	Antonym	Sentence
courageous	*cowardly*	*The cowardly lion ran from the mouse.*
6. expensive		
7. early		
8. succeed		
9. generous		
10. enormous		

Use with textbook page 301.

> **REMEMBER** When you read, identify the main idea and details. The main idea is the most important idea in a text. The details are small pieces of information that support the main idea.

Read each paragraph. Then answer the questions that follow.

1. Washing your hands is good for your health. Many germs are spread through human contact. When you shake hands with someone, touch a doorknob, or borrow a pen, you can get germs on your hands. If you then touch your mouth or eyes, you spread the germs. Scrubbing with soap and water can take away the harmful germs.

   What is the main idea of the passage above?

   _____

   _____

2. What are the details that support the main idea?

   _____

   _____

3. Pasta is easy to make and fun to eat. Did you know that you can make it yourself? All it takes is flour, eggs and a pinch of salt. You take these ingredients and work them into a dough with your hands. Then you roll them out with a rolling pin. You can cut the dough into any shape you want. After you let it dry for a little while, you can cook it just like pasta from a box, except not quite as long. Look for a recipe and try it out!

   What is the main idea of the passage above?

   _____

   _____

4. What are the details that support the main idea?

   _____

   _____

5. How can identifying the main idea and details help you read with greater comprehension?

   _____

Name _____ Date _____

Choose the best answer for each item. Circle the letter of the correct answer.

1. The CSDR Cubs play against _____.

   a. only hearing impaired schools   **b.** only hearing schools   **c.** both hearing and hearing impaired schools

2. Before Coach Gonzales came, the team _____.

   a. had low morale and often lost   **b.** had high morale and often won   **c.** didn't even play games

3. In 2004, the CSDR team had a _____.

   a. losing record   **b.** winning record   **c.** tied record

4. The players communicate with _____.

   a. a spoken code   **b.** hand signals   **c.** coded messages to the cheerleaders

5. To congratulate the players, the fans _____.

   a. yell and scream   **b.** stamp their feet   **c.** raise their arms and wiggle their fingers

EXTENSION *Use with textbook page 307.*

Pick five words or phrases and write them below. Then research how to express them in American Sign Language. Write a description of the ASL gesture in the right-hand column. Then practice the Sign Language gesture with a classmate. Can you form a simple sentence using only your hands?

English	Description of ASL Gesture
applause	*arms straight up in air, wiggle fingers*

GRAMMAR, USAGE, AND MECHANICS

Present Perfect with *for* and *since* *Use with textbook page 308.*

REMEMBER The present perfect is formed with *have* or *has* + the past participle of a verb. It describes an action that began in the past and continues into the present.
When *for* is used with the present perfect, it describes a period of time that began in the past.
Example: She has played the piano for two years.
When *since* is used with the present perfect, it specifies the exact point in time when an activity began.
Example: She *has practiced* this composition *since January*.
Use adverbs such as *always, often, ever, never,* and *recently* to talk about when or how often something happened in the past.
Example: Have you ever seen a full moon? No, I never have.

Circle the correct adverb to complete each sentence.

Example: Our school has ((recently)/so far) hired a new soccer coach.

1. Our local soccer team has (always/ever) played well.

2. The team has (often/so far) won the championship game.

Answer each question below, using the present perfect with *for* or *since*.

Example: How long has he played football? (for)

He has played football for two seasons.

3. How long has she taken dance lessons? (since)

_____

4. How long have they planned the party? (for)

_____

5. How long has he dreamed of attending college? (since)

_____

WRITING a PERSUASIVE PARAGRAPH

Write a Letter to the Editor *Use with textbook page 309.*

This is the word web that Ari completed before writing his paragraph.

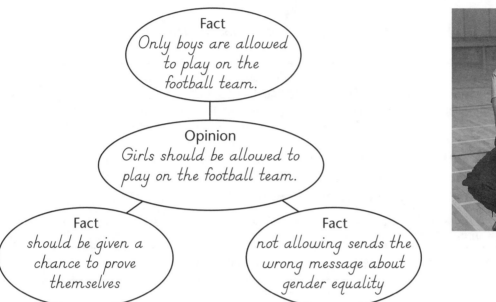

Fact
Only boys are allowed to play on the football team.

Opinion
Girls should be allowed to play on the football team.

Fact
should be given a chance to prove themselves

Fact
not allowing sends the wrong message about gender equality

Complete your own word web about an issue you feel strongly about in your school or community.

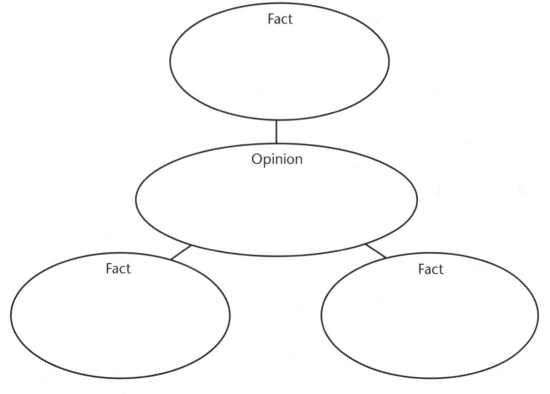

Fact

Opinion

Fact

Fact

What is the human spirit?

READING 4: From *The Diary of Anne Frank: The Play*

VOCABULARY **Literary Words** *Use with textbook page 311.*

> **REMEMBER** A **drama** is a play that is performed by actors. It consists of dialogue and **stage directions**. Stage directions describe the action and environment onstage. They are often printed in italics or brackets. A **diary** is a book in which you write about your own life and thoughts.

Read each sentence in the chart. Imagine that you are reading the diary of someone your age. Write *diary* if you think the sentence comes from a diary. Write *fiction* if you think the sentence is from a work of fiction.

Diary or Work of Fiction?	Description
fiction	Paula held the jewel up to the light.
1.	The earth is hollow inside.
2.	We spent the day playing at the park, and I had a great time.
3.	I think Andrea is feeling better this week.

Read the following excerpt from a play.

> DON: [*angrily*] Give it back, Rob! I'm warning you.
>
> ROB: Don, you know I didn't take Cathy's letter. [*Sighing*] I would never do that.
>   [*Rob reaches out a hand to Don, who refuses to take it.*]
>
> DON: Well if you didn't take it, who did? The cat?
>   [*Rob's cat walks across the stage in a purple spotlight. They watch it go.*]
>
> ROB: Somehow I doubt it, Donnie.
>   [*After a moment they both smile.*]

4. Underline the names of the speakers, and circle the stage directions.

5. Write two more lines of dialogue for the scene between Don and Rob.

_____

_____

VOCABULARY   **Academic Words**   *Use with textbook page 312.*

Read the paragraph below. Pay attention to the underlined academic words.

> Our school has <u>published</u> a student handbook for new students. The handbook has information about the school and lists <u>regulations</u> that students must obey. It also lists rules about how to behave when entering and leaving school. For example, we are not supposed to make noise in front of the school, as this would disturb the <u>occupants</u> of the apartment building next door. Though the handbook contains a lot of information, it has <u>assisted</u> many new students in adjusting to our school.

Write the academic words from the paragraph above next to their correct definitions.

Example: _*regulations*_ : official rules or orders

1. _____: helped someone

2. _____: printed and distributed

3. _____: people who live in a building, room, etc.

Use the academic words from the exercise above to complete the sentences.

4. Her new book is going to be _____ next month.

5. The tutor _____ me with my homework.

6. The _____ of the apartment weren't home when we visited.

7. In the lab, it's important to follow safety _____ so you don't get hurt.

Complete the sentences with your own ideas.

Example: The older students have assisted the _*incoming freshman*_.

8. If I ever write a book that is published, it will probably be about

_____.

9. The occupants of my home are _____.

10. In my school there are important regulations to follow, such as

_____.

REMEMBER The sound /j/ can be spelled *j* as in *jam*, *g* as in *gentle*, or *dge* as in *ledge*. The letter *j* is usually used before *a, o,* or *u.* The letter *g* is usually used before *e, i,* or *y.* The letters *dge* are often used when the sound comes at the end of a syllable or word. Knowing these patterns can help you spell and pronounce the words correctly.

Read the words in the box below. Then write each word in the correct column in the chart.

project	lodge	general	acknowledge	jacket
wedge	Japan	giraffe	gym	

/j/ spelled *j*	/j/ spelled *g*	/j/ spelled *dge*
project		

Write the pattern for /j/ in each word below.

Example: bridge _____*/j/ spelled dge*_____

1. genuine _____

2. reject _____

3. energy _____

4. pledge _____

5. January _____

6. giant _____

7. journal _____

READING STRATEGY **READ ALOUD** *Use with textbook page 313.*

> **REMEMBER** Learning to read aloud brings a story and characters to life.

Read each passage. Then answer the questions.

Lucy: Remember when we had that big fight?
Jenna: I'm sorry about that. I didn't mean those things I said.
Lucy: I forgive you, because it's important to forgive your friends, right?
Jenna: Right!
Lucy: Then I hope you'll forgive me, because I just crashed your bike.

1. If you were reading Jenna's first line, what emotion would you show?

_____

_____

2. If you were reading Lucy's last line, what emotion would you show?

_____

_____

Dad: You can't go to the party and that's final.
Raymond: But you said I could go!
Dad: That's before I found out that the party is 100 miles away!
Raymond: That's so unfair!

3. If you were reading Dad's lines, what emotion would be in your voice?

_____

4. How does the punctuation in this passage help you to know how to read Raymond's lines?

_____

_____

5. How do you think the strategy of reading aloud with expression will make you a better reader?

_____

_____

Choose the best answer for each item. Circle the letter of the correct answer.

1. The Franks moved into the Secret Annex when _____.

   a. the Germans invaded Holland and the Dutch surrendered
   b. Anne's sister was ordered to work in Germany
   c. Anne turned sixteen

2. The Franks were hidden by _____.

   a. two former work colleagues
   b. Peter van Daan and his family
   c. the secret police

3. When Peter arrives, Anne feels quite _____.

   a. worried
   b. protective of her space
   c. excited

4. While Anne is positive and upbeat, the adults are _____.

   a. nervous
   b. arguing
   c. bored

5. Reading a play rather than a diary allows you to experience _____.

   a. a nonfiction account
   b. one person's voice
   c. many points of view

RESPONSE TO LITERATURE *Use with textbook page 323.*

Anne Frank hid in a tiny annex with her family for two years. They couldn't walk the streets or make too much noise, and lived on very little food. They lived in fear of capture. Try to imagine living in those conditions. In the space below, write a short paragraph describing how that might feel.

_____

_____

_____

_____

_____

GRAMMAR, USAGE, AND MECHANICS

Simple Past versus Present Perfect *Use with textbook page 324.*

REMEMBER The simple past describes an action that happened and was completed at a specific time in the past. The simple past of regular verbs is formed by adding *-ed* or *-d* to the base form. The simple past of irregular verbs must be memorized.
Example: She traveled to California last year.
The present perfect describes an action that occurred at an indefinite time in the past or an action that began in the past and continues into the present. It is formed with *has* or *have* and the past participle of a verb.
Example: He *has traveled* through fifteen states.

Circle the correct verb form in each sentence below.

Example: My family ((moved)/ has moved) to California in 1999.

1. We (saw / have seen) the Grand Canyon last summer.

2. You (enjoyed / have enjoyed) that game ever since you first played it.

Complete the sentences, using your own ideas. Be sure to use the simple past or the present perfect correctly.

Example: I have agreed _*to help my father this weekend.*_

3. We started _____

4. The students in my school have created _____

5. My teacher looked _____

WRITING A PERSUASIVE PARAGRAPH

Write a Persuasive Paragraph *Use with textbook page 325.*

This is the pros-and-cons chart that George completed before writing his paragraph.

Pros	Cons
Publishing helps millions of readers to better understand the tragedy of war. Editing personal passages respects Anne's privacy	Publishing private thoughts disrespects Anne's privacy. Editing any passages is wrong.

Complete your own pros-and-cons chart for a paragraph on an issue you feel strongly about.

Pros	Cons

EDIT AND PROOFREAD   Use with textbook page 332.

Read the paragraph below carefully. Look for mistakes in spelling, punctuation, and grammar. Mark the mistakes with editing marks (textbook page 460). Then rewrite the paragraph correctly on the lines below.

I have been going to the park every day to practice tennis. I play on the varsity team, but everyone needs practice. One day, after I had been Practicing for about an hour, I saw my grandad sitting at one of the picnic benches. He was sitting all alone, and he looked sad. After I finished practicing, I walked over to his bench and asked how he was doing. Granddad just grinned. "Do you play chess" he asked. I has played a few times. He asked if I wanted to play a game. we played three games of chess that afternoon. I came close to beeting him once but he smiled and captured one of my pieces right away After our last game I said goodbye and walked back to the tennis cort.

_____

_____

_____

_____

_____

_____

_____

_____

_____

_____

Underline the vocabulary items you know and can use well. Review and practice any you haven't underlined. Underline them when you know them well.

Literary Words	Key Words	Academic Words	
dialogue	chemicals	founded	participate
theme	crops	impact	perceive
diary	demand	labor	prior
drama	migrant workers	persistence	team
stage directions	strike	academic	assisted
	union	policy	occupants
	accomplish	principal	published
	mission	tradition	regulations
	hearing impaired		
	obstacle		
	opponent		
	sign language		

Put a check by the skills you can perform well. Review and practice any you haven't checked off. Check them off when you can perform them well.

Skills	I can . . .
Word Study	☐ recognize and spell capitalized words. ☐ recognize and spell words ending with consonant + *-le, -al,* and *-el.* ☐ recognize antonyms. ☐ recognize and spell words with the /j/ sound.
Reading Strategies	☐ distinguish fact from opinion. ☐ make inferences. ☐ identify the main idea and details. ☐ read aloud.
Grammar, Usage, and Mechanics	☐ use inseparable phrasal verbs. ☐ use punctuation in quotations. ☐ use the present perfect with *for* and *since.* ☐ use the simple past or the present perfect.
Writing	☐ write an advertisement. ☐ write a review of a book, film, or play. ☐ write a letter to the editor. ☐ write a persuasive paragraph. ☐ write an expository essay.

Learn about Art with the Smithsonian
American Art Museum *Use with textbook pages 334–335.*

LEARNING TO LOOK

Look at *Spirit of Life* by Daniel Chester French on page 335 in your textbook.
Describe six things you see in this sculpture. State facts, not opinions.

Example: *The figure has wings.*

1. _____

2. _____

3. _____

4. _____

5. _____

6. _____

INTERPRETATION

Look at *Fan Quilt, Mt. Carmel* by the Residents of Bourbon County, Kentucky, on
page 334 in your textbook. Imagine that you are helping them to make the quilt.
Recreate a conversation they might have had. Include yourself as a character!

Example: *This is so time consuming, but I love to sew with different colors.*

_____

_____

_____

_____

_____

_____

KWLH

Look at *Speaking to Hear* by Michael Olszewski on page 335 in your textbook. Use that artwork to complete the KWLH Chart below.

K	W	L	H
What do you **know** about using fabric in art?	What do you **want** to learn about this work of art?	What have you **learned** about using fabric in art from looking at this work?	**How** have you learned about fabric in art?

Name _____ Date _____

How does the sky influence us?

READING 1: "Starry Nights" / "Stars" / "Escape at Bedtime"

VOCABULARY **Literary Words** *Use with textbook page 339.*

REMEMBER A **stanza** is a group of lines in a poem, usually similar in length and pattern. Stanzas are sparated by spaces. **Rhyme** is the repetition of sounds at the ends of words. The lines in a stanza sometimes rhyme.

Read each pair of lines. Write *yes* if the lines rhyme. Write *no* if the lines do not rhyme. (Words with similar spellings may not have the same sound.)

Rhyme?	Lines
yes	The snow is very nice But I detest the ice
1.	Lush as a peach, twice as smooth
2.	The passing of time is quick and sublime
3.	Her love was a lamp Illuminating my heart
4.	Alone, in despair He sat in his chair

5. Write a stanza of a poem that has four rhyming lines.

_____

_____

_____

_____

Read the paragraph below. Pay attention to the underlined academic words.

> Jackson Pollock was a famous painter. He didn't paint realistic <u>images</u> of people, places, or things. He created paintings by pouring and dripping paint all over a canvas placed on the floor. Each drip and splash is a <u>visible</u> record of how he created the picture. Many art lovers and critics have tried to <u>analyze</u> the meaning behind Pollock's work. One <u>interpretation</u> is that it represents the artist's need to let go and create freely.

Write the letter of the correct definition next to each word.

Example: ___c___ analyze

_____ **1.** interpretation

_____ **2.** visible

_____ **3.** image

a. something that can be seen

b. a picture that you can see through a camera, on a television, in a mirror, etc.

c. examine or think about something carefully in order to understand it

d. an explanation of the meaning or significance of something

Use the academic words from the exercise above to complete the sentences.

4. The _____ on the movie screen was twenty feet high.

5. Each witness gave a different _____ of what he had heard.

6. We had terrible seats, and the stage was barely _____ from that part of the theater.

7. The scientists took three months to _____ the data from the satellite.

Complete the sentences with your own ideas.

Example: His stories analyze the way people _*show their love*_____.

8. I'll always remember the image of _____.

9. What is your interpretation of _____?

10. The _____ is visible from my home.

Name _____ Date _____

WORD STUDY   **Lexical Sets** *Use with textbook page 341.*

REMEMBER Words that describe one main idea are called *lexical sets*. For instance, the lexical set for *easy* can include *simple, effortless, straightforward,* and *uncomplicated.* Knowing lexical sets can help you use the precise word you need to convey your meaning.

Look at the chart below. Underline the word that is _not_ part of the lexical set. Use a dictionary if needed.

Word	Word	Word	Word
common	familiar	usual	<u>exotic</u>
1. casual	formal	mellow	easygoing
2. surprising	startling	unanticipated	predictable
3. clean	spotless	tidy	grimy
4. sour	tart	sugary	bitter
5. interesting	dull	appealing	fascinating

Write two or more words for each lexical set. Use a dictionary or thesaurus if needed.

Example: difficult *hard, tough* _____

6. exciting _____

7. unusual _____

8. cheap _____

9. nice _____

10. boring _____

> **REMEMBER** Connecting ideas in different texts helps you get different perspectives on a topic. To connect ideas among texts, look for the most important idea in each text and compare them.

Read the poems by Christina Rossetti. Then answer the questions.

53

If stars dropped out of heaven,
And if flowers took their place,
The sky would still look very fair,
And fair earth's face.

Winged angels might fly down to us
To pluck the stars,
But we would only long for flowers
Beyond the cloudy bars.

55

What do the stars do
Up in the sky,
Higher than the wind can blow,
Or the clouds can fly?

Each star in it's own glory
Circles, circles still;
As it was lit to shine and set,
And do its Maker's will.

1. What is the most important idea in the first poem? _____

    _____

2. What is the most important idea in the second poem? _____

    _____

3. How are the poems similar? _____

    _____

4. What different perspectives about stars do the poems give you? _____

    _____

5. How can the strategy of connecting ideas help you get different perspectives on a topic?

    _____

Name _____ Date _____

Choose the best answer for each item. Circle the letter of the correct answer.

1. Van Gogh felt that most paintings of nighttime scenes did not capture night's _____.

   a. loudness **b.** darkness **c.** colors

2. Unlike many other painters who worked on nighttime scenes, van Gogh _____.

   a. painted at night **b.** used mainly **c.** painted in daylight
   black paint

3. In the poem "Stars," Sara Teasdale describes the stars as _____.

   a. friendly and close **b.** angry and fearsome **c.** distant and amazing

4. The final stanza of Teasdale's poem focuses on _____.

   a. an early morning sky **b.** a city cafe at night **c.** the way stars make
   her feel

5. In "Escape at Bedtime," Stevenson rhymes every _____.

   a. two lines **b.** three lines **c.** four lines

RESPONSE TO LITERATURE *Use with textbook page 347.*

Van Gogh's description of a café at night is found on page 343 of your textbook. Read his description again. Then draw your own interpretation of what van Gogh saw there.

GRAMMAR, USAGE, AND MECHANICS

Punctuation in Prose and Poetry *Use with textbook page 348.*

> **REMEMBER** In prose, or regular written language, you must always capitalize the first letter of the first word in every sentence. Names and the personal pronoun *I* are capitalized as well. Every sentence ends with a punctuation mark such as a period, an exclamation mark, or a question mark.
> In poetry, punctuation does not follow these rules. Instead, it often becomes part of the poet's creative style.

Read the sentences. Add the correct punctuation following each punctuation rule for prose. Circle all letters that should be capitalized, and add punctuation marks.

Example: ⓟlease turn off the light when you leave the room!

1. you are late

2. why did you not come earlier

3. i saw thomas yesterday

4. we couldn't see much in the darkness therefore we stood completely still

5. help

Rewrite the poem as prose. Use the correct punctuation.

little by little
    the tiny child walked
through
     the
       field

finding
    a wishflower
she blew on it
sending its seeds far and wide
    like little parachutes of hope

_____

_____

_____

_____

Name _____ Date _____

WRITE A RESEARCH REPORT

Write an Introductory Paragraph *Use with textbook page 349.*

This is the inverted pyramid that Ari completed before conducting his research.

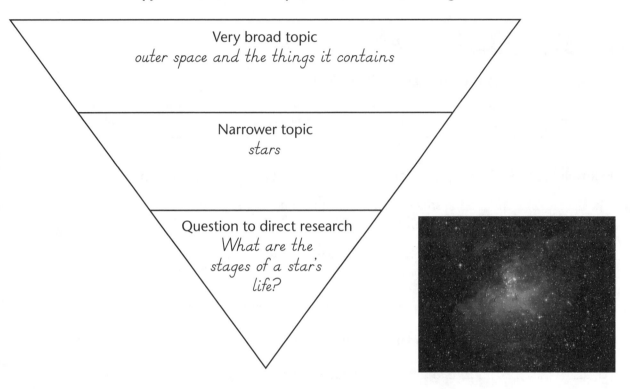

Very broad topic
outer space and the things it contains

Narrower topic
stars

Question to direct research
What are the stages of a star's life?

Complete your own inverted pyramid to narrow your topic down to a single researchable question.

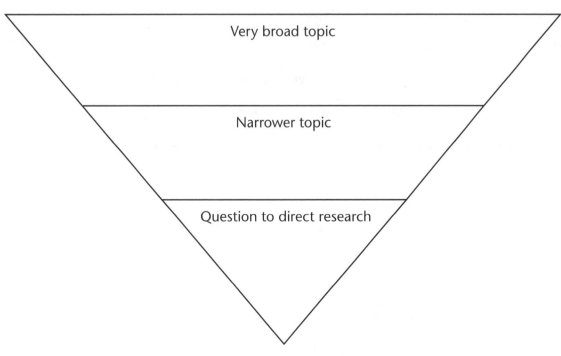

Very broad topic

Narrower topic

Question to direct research

READING 2: "Earth and the Milky Way"

VOCABULARY **Key Words** *Use with textbook page 351.*

Write each word in the box next to its definition.

asteroids	comet	gravity	meteoroids	orbit	planets

Example: _____*asteroids*_____: large objects made of rock that move around in space

1. _____: small objects that produce a bright burning line in the sky when they travel in space

2. _____: an object in the sky like a very bright ball with a tail that moves through space

3. _____: the path traveled by an object moving around a larger object

4. _____: very large round objects in space that move around a star

5. _____: the force of attraction between objects in the universe

Use the words in the box at the top of the page to complete the sentences.

6. There are eight _____ in our solar system.

7. These planets all _____ the sun.

8. The force of _____ is stronger on Jupiter than on Earth.

9. A line across the night sky might be caused by a distant _____.

10. Dinosaurs may have died when a large _____ crashed into the earth.

Name _____ Date _____

Read the paragraph below. Pay attention to the underlined academic words.

NASA chose the first seven astronauts in 1959 from a select group of people recommended by the United States military. Now anyone with an education that <u>features</u> a strong background in math and science can apply. One does, though, also have to satisfy the strict mental and physical health <u>criteria</u>. The Astronaut Candidate training program is <u>located</u> in Houston, TX. The program lasts two years and training <u>consists</u> of studying manuals, learning computer systems, and spending time in flight simulators.

Write the academic words from the paragraph above next to their correct definitions.

Example: ___*located*___ : in a particular place or position

1. _____: facts or standards used in order to help you judge or decide something

2. _____: is made of or contains a number of different things

3. _____: important, interesting, or typical parts of something

Use the academic words from the paragraph above to complete the sentences.

4. The salesman showed us some interesting _____ of the car.

5. The mysterious object _____ of ice and rock.

6. The world's largest ball of string is _____ in England.

7. That letter to the editor didn't meet the _____ needed to be printed in the paper.

Complete the sentences with your own ideas.

Example: One of my favorite features on the new car is ___*the great stereo*___.

8. My neighborhood is located in _____.

9. One of my criteria for making new friends is _____.

10. My dinner usually consists of _____.

Use with textbook page 353.

> **REMEMBER** Many English words are based on Greek and Latin roots such as *astro* (star), *ology* (study of), and *geo* (earth). Knowing these Greek and Latin roots can help you define many words.

Look at the chart below. Define each word based on the meaning of its root. Use a dictionary if needed.

Root	Meaning	Word	Meaning
geo	*earth*	geothermal	*heat from inside the earth*
1. geo		geology	
2. ology		mythology	
3. ology		ecology	
4. astro		asteroid	
5. astro		asterisk	

Underline the Greek or Latin root in each word. Then write the definition of each word based on the meaning of its root. Use a dictionary to check your work.

Example: zo<u>ology</u>   *study of animals*

6. geologist   _____

7. biology   _____

8. geometry   _____

9. anthropology   _____

10. astronomical   _____

READING STRATEGY | **USE VISUALS** *Use with textbook page 353.*

> **REMEMBER** Using visuals helps you better understand a text. Visuals can be art, photographs, diagrams, charts, and maps. Ask yourself what the visual shows and how it can help understand the reading.

Read the passage. Then answer the questions that follow.

On July 20, 1969, Neil Armstrong became the first person to touch the surface of the moon. As he walked the moon's surface, he said, "That's one small step for man; one giant leap for mankind." With fellow pilot Buzz Aldrin, Armstrong took photographs and collected soil samples. He described the moon's surface as being like powdered charcoal.

1. What is the passage above about?

   _____

2. What does the picture show?

   _____

3. How does the picture help you understand Armstrong and Aldrin's moon landing?

   _____

4. What does the picture tell you that the text does not?

   _____

5. How can using visuals help you better understand what you are reading?

   _____

Choose the best answer for each item. Circle the letter of the correct answer.

1. In our solar system, there are _____.

   a. six planets   **b.** seven planets   **c.** eight planets

2. The sun is a _____.

   a. huge asteroid   **b.** medium-sized star   **c.** galaxy of meteors

3. In our solar system, Jupiter is the biggest _____.

   a. dwarf star   **b.** moon   **c.** planet

4. Comets consist of _____.

   a. stone and metal   **b.** ice and dust   **c.** gas and meteors

5. The force that keeps stars together is _____.

   a. gravity   **b.** magnetism   **c.** heat

EXTENSION *Use with textbook page 363.*

The objects in our solar system were discovered long ago. Research stars and planets. When were they discovered?

Star or planet	Date of discovery
Saturn	1610

Name _____ Date _____

GRAMMAR, USAGE, AND MECHANICS

Noun/Pronoun Agreement *Use with textbook page 364.*

REMEMBER Pronouns such as *he* or *they* can refer to or replace a single noun or a noun phrase, when the noun or noun phrase is the subject (the person or thing performing the action) of the sentence. When the noun or noun phrase is the object (the person or thing receiving the action) of the sentence, use object pronouns such as *him* and *them*.
Example: Peter doesn't like his apartment. He wants to move. Sandra will help him find a new place. The pronoun must agree in gender and number with the noun it replaces.

Read the passage. Circle all singular pronouns. Underline all plural pronouns.

　　Andrew and Ginger met at a party in New York. (He) was immediately struck by her beauty. He watched her all night. Andrew's friends noticed that he was absent-minded. They asked him if something was wrong. Andrew shook his head, but wouldn't take his eyes off the beautiful creature. She fascinated him.

Replace the underlined word(s) in the paragraph with the correct pronoun.

　　Kristy and I arrived at the ballpark early so we could watch batting practice. Kristy was very excited. <u>Kristy</u> had never been to a baseball game before. We had great seats
_(Example)
too. Kristy was awestruck at how close we were to the field. "The players are so close!"
<u>Kristy</u> exclaimed. One of <u>the players</u> even gave <u>Kristy</u> a souvenir baseball. Best of all, he
₍₁₎ 　　　　　　　　　₍₂₎　　　　　　　₍₃₎
autographed <u>the baseball</u> for her! <u>Kristy and I</u> had a great time at the ballpark that day.
　　　　　　　₍₄₎　　　　　　　₍₅₎

Example: ___She___

1. _____　　　　4. _____

2. _____　　　　5. _____

3. _____

WRITING A RESEARCH REPORT

Support the Main Idea *Use with textbook page 365.*

This is the main-idea-and-details web that Pablo completed before writing his paragraph.

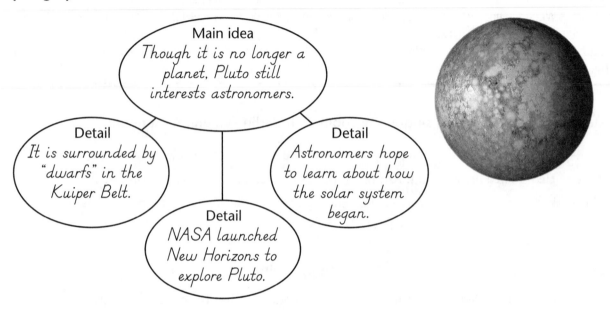

Main idea
Though it is no longer a planet, Pluto still interests astronomers.

Detail
It is surrounded by "dwarfs" in the Kuiper Belt.

Detail
NASA launched New Horizons to explore Pluto.

Detail
Astronomers hope to learn about how the solar system began.

Complete your own main-idea-and-details web for a paragraph that includes a main idea and supporting details.

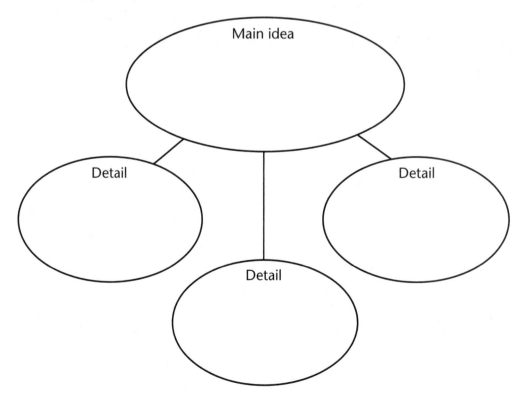

Main idea

Detail

Detail

Detail

How does the sky influence us?

UNIT 6

READING 3: "The Girl Who Married the Moon"

VOCABULARY **Literary Words** *Use with textbook page 367.*

REMEMBER A **myth** is a short fictional tale that explains the origins of elements of nature. It has been passed from generation to generation by storytellers. Sometimes myths use **personification**, which gives human qualities to nonhuman animals or things.

Read each sentence. Write *yes* if it uses personification. Write *no* if it does not use personification.

Personification?	Sentences
yes	The house stood watchfully at the end of the lane.
1.	The roof pointed toward the sky.
2.	The city came alive, stretching its limbs, beginning to speak morning words.
3.	There's a sense of humor to the moonlight tonight. It's as if the moon wants us to stay out a little later.

Read the short myth and answer the questions that follow.

> The face of the moon is a mirror. It's carried across the sky by a family, whose skin is so pale and delicate that they can only come out at night, so they don't get burned. The family members pull the moon across the sky. They look at Earth in the mirror. That way they remember where they came from. The <u>smiling face</u> in the moon belongs to the person carrying the moon. The stars twinkle at them in greeting. And the ocean waters wave and say hello when the moon floats by.

4. Underline the words and phrases that personify nonhuman objects or animals.

5. What natural phenomena does the myth try to explain?

_____

_____

Read the paragraph below. Pay attention to the underlined academic words.

My first <u>job</u> was babysitting for a family with two children named Haley and Jack. Haley was still a baby, and her parents <u>instructed</u> me how to change her diaper. I was told their older child Jack was <u>restricted</u> from watching television after 8:00 P.M. Jack did not like when I told him it was time to go to bed. He <u>ignored</u> me and kept watching television. The first night babysitting was hard.

Write the letter of the correct definition next to each word.

Example: ___*d*___ job

_____ **1.** ignored

_____ **2.** instructed

_____ **3.** restricted

a. did not pay attention to someone or something

b. not allowed to do something

c. taught or showed someone how to do something

d. a particular duty or responsibility that you have

Use the academic words from the exercise above to complete the sentences.

4. Our grandmother _____ us how to play the game of bridge.

5. The protesters were _____ from entering the building.

6. His boring summer _____ was not much fun.

7. Danielle _____ the invitation from her friends since she had to work.

Complete the sentences with your own ideas.

Example: ___*My dad*_____ instructed me to get out of bed early.

8. I ignored the _____ outside.

9. My ideal job would be _____.

10. Because I'm not an adult, I'm restricted from _____.

WORD STUDY   Spelling Long *i* *Use with textbook page 369.*

> **REMEMBER** The long *i* sound can be spelled several different ways. These include *i_e* as in *side*, *igh* as in *tight*, *y* as in *my*, and *i* as in *kind*. Knowing these patterns will help you spell words with the long *i* sound correctly.

Read the words in the box below. Then write each word in the correct column in the chart.

while	style	isle	tonight	worthwhile	supply
grind	tightly	versatile	blind	blight	July

Long i spelled *i_e*	Long i spelled *igh*	Long i spelled *y*	Long i spelled *i*
while			

Write the letter-sound pattern for long *i* in each word below.

Example: might *long /i/ spelled igh*

13. island _____

14. sign _____

15. slice _____

16. simplify _____

17. sprite _____

18. sigh _____

19. rind _____

20. unify _____

> **REMEMBER** When you read for enjoyment, you aren't just reading for information. You are reading to be entertained by other things, such as the characters, the setting, or the pictures that go with the text.

Read the passage. Then answer the questions that follow.

Anne of Green Gables is one of the most famous fictional characters in literature. One of the best things about her is that she is not perfect. She has several things she can't stand about herself, including her plain name (she adds the "e" to the end of "Ann" to make it seem fancier) and her bright red hair. She is always getting in trouble. But although the book was published in 1908, it is still popular. In fact, thousands of people still visit Canada's Prince Edward Island just to see where Anne was supposed to live!

1. What qualities do you think make a great character?

_____

_____

2. Who is your favorite fictional character? Why?

_____

_____

3. What is your favorite setting in a novel or story you've read?

_____

_____

4. What is the name of the book that you have most enjoyed reading? Why?

_____

_____

5. When you read for pleasure, what sorts of texts do you choose to read? Write the name of one book you would like to read for pleasure.

_____

_____

Name _____ Date _____

COMPREHENSION *Use with textbook page 378.*

Choose the best answer for each item. Circle the letter of the correct answer.

1. The two cousins could have married almost anyone but they fell in love with _____.

   a. the stars   **b.** the sun   **c.** the moon

2. The Moon wanted a wife who was very _____.

   a. patient   **b.** pretty   **c.** quiet

3. After awhile, the Moon's wife became _____.

   a. bored   **b.** sad   **c.** content

4. The people lying facedown on the trail were _____.

   a. suns   **b.** stars   **c.** more moons

5. The Moon decided to let his wife _____.

   a. rest at home   **b.** carry pieces of moon   **c.** watch the sun rise with him

RESPONSE TO LITERATURE *Use with textbook page 379.*

Find a chart showing the moon in orbit around the earth. What part of the lunar cycle is carried by the Moon? What part is carried by his wife? Draw your own diagram to show the answers.

GRAMMAR, USAGE, AND MECHANICS

Modal Verb: _must_   _Use with textbook page 380._

> **REMEMBER**   Like all modal verbs, _must_ is always used with other verbs to add information. _Must_ can express obligation (**Example:** I must _work_ every day.), necessity (**Example:** I must _have_ coffee every morning to wake up.), strong advice (**Example:** You must _take_ your medicine.), or certainty (**Example:** You must _be kidding_.). _Must not_ expresses what is prohibited or forbidden (**Example:** You must not _park_ here.).
>
> _Must_ does not change its form depending on tense or person and does not use _do/don't_ with its negative form or questions.

Rewrite each sentence, replacing the underlined verb with _must_ or _must not_.

Example: He <u>has to</u> go to work early today.

He must go to work early today.

1. You <u>are not allowed to</u> smoke in restaurants.

_____

2. I am sure he has not forgotten about me. He <u>will probably be</u> late.

_____

3. You <u>should</u> wear sunscreen to protect your skin.

_____

Write your own sentences using the modal verbs _must_ or _must not_.

Example: Express necessity.

I must eat something before I get too hungry to do my schoolwork.

4. Express obligation.

_____

5. Express strong advice.

_____

WRITING A RESEARCH REPORT

Include Paraphrases and Citations *Use with textbook page 381.*

This is the source chart that Madeline completed to manage her citations.

Paraphrase	Source
According to the myth, when a solar eclipse occurs, it's because a black squirrel is eating the sun. Therefore, whenever the Choctaw saw a black squirrel, they would try to frighten it away, hoping to protect the sun.	"Eclipse of the Sun Blamed on Black Squirrel." Choctaw Legends and Stories. 13 September 2007. http://www.tc.umn.edu/~mboucher/mikebouchweb/Choctaw/legends2.htm.

Complete your own source chart listing citations for a paragraph about a myth.

Paraphrase	Source

READING 4: "Return to the Moon" / "No Need to Establish a Moon Base"

VOCABULARY **Key Words** *Use with textbook page 383.*

Write each word in the box next to its definition.

base	crater	lunar	mine	universe	voyage

Example: _____*mine*_____ : dig into the ground in order to get gold, coal, etc.

1. _____ : all of space, including the stars and planets

2. _____ : a round hole in the ground made by something that has fallen or exploded

3. _____ : relating to the moon

4. _____ : a long trip, especially in a ship or space vehicle

5. _____ : a shelter or headquarters from which an exploration can depart

Use the words in the box at the top of the page to complete the sentences.

6. The phases of the moon are known as the _____ cycle.

7. A journey across the known _____ might take trillions of years.

8. The hikers established their _____ at the bottom of the mountain.

9. Developers _____ in areas where they know coal exists.

10. The ship's captain was looking forward to the _____.

VOCABULARY **Academic Words** *Use with textbook page 384.*

Read the paragraph below. Pay attention to the underlined academic words.

> NASA, the National Aeronautics and Space Agency, uses telescopes and spacecraft to <u>investigate</u> our solar system and beyond. NASA scientists <u>research</u> important <u>issues</u> related to Earth, other planets, and the universe. NASA also works to <u>promote</u> public interest in its space programs. It has an excellent website with amazing photographs of the universe.

Write the academic words from the paragraph above next to their correct definitions.

Example: ___*research*___ : serious study of a subject that is intended to discover new facts about it

1. _____ : help something develop and be successful

2. _____ : subjects or problems that people discuss

3. _____ : try to find out the truth about something

Use the academic words from the paragraph above to complete the sentences.

4. The group deals with major social _____ like poverty and health care.

5. Alex put up flyers to _____ his new band.

6. The detective began to _____ the crime scene.

7. Sawyer is doing _____ on the way fruit flies balance in the air.

Complete the sentences with your own ideas.

Example: Smoky the Bear promotes ___*forest safety*___ .

8. Two important issues facing young people today are

_____ .

9. I would like to investigate _____ .

10. In school I'm doing research on _____ .

REMEMBER Acronyms are created by using the first letters of a phrase, as in *LCD*, liquid crystal display. The letters are usually all capitalized and do not have periods between them.

Read each acronym. Then use a dictionary to find out what it stands for. Write the phrase in the chart.

Acronym	Words that Form Acronym
PIN	*Personal Identification Number*
1. NASA	
2. ATM	
3. FAQ	
4. CEO	
5. WWW	

Write the definition of each acronym. Use a dictionary if needed.

Example: UFO *unidentified flying object*

6. ZIP (code) _____

7. TLC _____

8. Sonar _____

9. FYI _____

10. VIP _____

READING STRATEGY | **TAKE NOTES** | *Use with textbook page 385.*

> **REMEMBER** Taking notes helps you understand and remember new information. Think about your purpose for reading when you take notes. Scan the text and look for the information you need. Don't write in complete sentences.

Read each passage. Then answer the questions that follow.

Zebra finches make great pets. They are small birds that are lively and fun to watch as they fly around in their cages. Their peeps and chirps are quieter than the piercing sound of parrots. Unlike some larger birds that need room to fly around in your house, zebra finches are happy to live in their cages all the time. But owning pets is a big responsibility. Zebra finches need a fairly large cage. They need companionship, so you should buy a pair of them. They need fresh water for drinking and bathing and fresh finch seed. They also like fruits and vegetables.

1. Set a purpose for reading the passage. What do you hope to learn from it?

_____

_____

2. Take notes from the passage above.

_____

_____

3. What are the three most important facts in the text?

_____

_____

4. Write one question you have about the information presented in the passage.

_____

_____

5. Why is the strategy of taking notes important to understanding and remembering what you read?

_____

_____

Choose the best answer for each item. Circle the letter of the correct answer.

1. Scientists believe that the moon was originally _____.

   a. part of the sun   **b.** another planet   **c.** part of earth

2. A moon base might allow astronauts to _____.

   a. study the way   **b.** study the moon and the   **c.** learn more about the
   asteroids move   rest of the universe   nearby planet Venus

3. NASA wants colonies of astronauts to eventually live on the moon for _____.

   a. as long as six weeks   **b.** as long as six months   **c.** as long as six years

4. Compared to manned space missions, robotic missions are _____.

   a. more dangerous   **b.** much safer   **c.** about equally safe

5. The two authors disagree _____.

   a. about how to   **b.** about how many space   **c.** if we should explore
   explore space   missions to fly   space further

Several countries have launched satellites in the last 50 years. Research five countries and tell when they launched their first satellite.

Country	Date of first satellite launch
United States	*January 31, 1958*

GRAMMAR, USAGE, AND MECHANICS

Cause-and-Effect Structures *Use with textbook page 392.*

> **REMEMBER** *Because, so,* and *since* signal cause and effect.
> **Example:** It was too cold outside, so we stayed in all day. Because it was too cold outside, we stayed in all day.
> The clause stating the effect sometimes comes before the clause stating the cause.

Read each sentence. Write *C* or *E* in the space before the sentence to indicate whether the underlined clause is a cause or an effect.

Example: __*E*__ Space travel is dangerous, <u>so we should not continue the space program</u>.

_____ 1. We should send robots into space, <u>because they can perform most tasks more precisely than humans</u>.

_____ 2. <u>So humans can stay there for long periods of time</u>, the moon base would have to be stocked with many supplies.

_____ 3. The systems keeping humans alive in space cost too much money, <u>so we should find other ways to explore space</u>.

Complete the sentences below by adding *because, so* or *since*. Then underline the cause in each sentence and circle the effect.

Example: (We moved to a warmer climate) _____ *because* _____ <u>it is more pleasant</u>.

4. I work hard _____ that I can do well at school.

5. _____ you were late, I started eating dinner without you.

Include Quotations and Citations *Use with textbook page 393.*

This is the source chart that Andrew completed to manage his quotes and sources.

Quotation	Source
"Private companies in Russia, Europe, and the United States are competing to become future leaders of space tourism."	*All about Space Tourism." Space.com 25 October 2007. http://www.space.com/ space-tourism/*

Complete your own source chart for a paragraph that includes quotations and citations.

Quotation	Source

EDIT AND PROOFREAD *Use with textbook page 402.*

Read the paragraph carefully. Look for mistakes in spelling, punctuation, and grammar. Mark the mistakes with proofreader's marks (textbook page 460). Then rewrite the paragraph correctly on the lines.

This weak the eighth grade class took a field trip to the space Exploration museum. Hannah had been to the museum several times she really enjoyed the exhibits. She dreamed of growing up to become an astronaut. The group was passing a Display about Goddard's rockets when her phone rang Her mother was calling her. Hannah looked around for a place to anser the phone in private. She went to a hallway nearby so she wouldn't disturb any one. Our teacher got upset that Hannah left the group.

_____

_____

_____

_____

_____

_____

_____

_____

_____

_____

_____

Underline each vocabulary item you know and can use well. Review and practice any you haven't underlined. Underline them when you know them well.

Literary Words	Key Words	Academic Words	
stanza	asteroids	analyze	ignored
rhyme	comet	image	instructed
myth	gravity	interpretation	job
personification	meteoroids	visible	restricted
	orbit	consists	investigate
	planets	criteria	issues
	base	features	promote
	crater	located	research
	lunar		
	mine		
	universe		
	voyage		

Put a check by the skills you can perform well. Review and practice any you haven't checked off. Check them off when you can perform them well.

Skills	I can . . .
Word Study	☐ recognize and use lexical sets. ☐ recognize and use Greek and Latin roots. ☐ recognize and spell words with a long *i*. ☐ recognize words that form acronyms.
Reading Strategies	☐ connect ideas. ☐ use visuals. ☐ read for enjoyment. ☐ take notes.
Grammar, Usage, and Mechanics	☐ use punctuation in prose and poetry. ☐ use noun/pronoun agreement. ☐ use the modal verb *must*. ☐ use cause-and-effect structures.
Writing	☐ write an introductory paragraph for a research report. ☐ write a paragraph that includes a main idea and details. ☐ write a paragraph using paraphrases and citations. ☐ write a paragraph using quotations and citations. ☐ write an expository essay.

Learn about Art with the Smithsonian
American Art Museum *Use with textbook pages 404–405.*

LEARNING TO LOOK

Look at *Orion in December* by Charles Burchfield on page 405 in your textbook. The artist felt inspired to paint *Orion in December* after looking out of his bedroom window on a winter night. Pretend you are looking out of a bedroom window. How would you paint the same scene?

Example: *I would paint a winter night in December with snow . . .*

_____

_____

_____

_____

_____

_____

INTERPRETATION

Look at *The Eclipse* by Alma Thomas on page 404 in your textbook. If this painting could give off a sound, what would it be? Explain your answer.

Example: *The sound would be loud and made with drums.*

_____

_____

_____

_____

_____

Look again at *Orion in December* and *The Eclipse* again. Use these two artworks to complete the diagram below. Describe each piece of art in the outer sections of the diagram. Then list the similarities between the two paintings in the center where the two circles overlap.

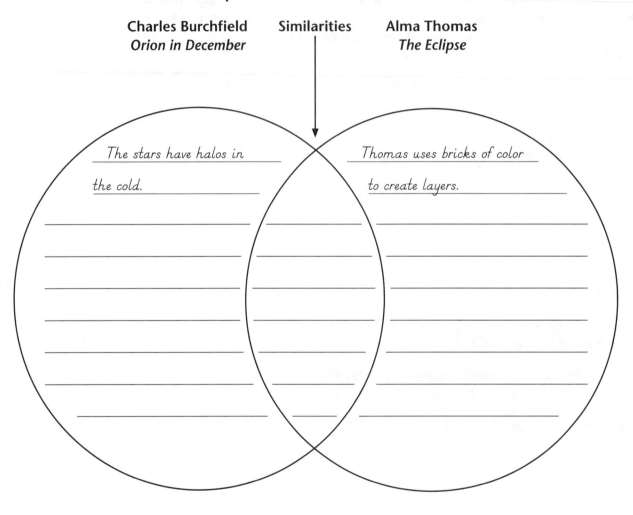

Charles Burchfield
Orion in December

Similarities

Alma Thomas
The Eclipse

The stars have halos in the cold.

Thomas uses bricks of color to create layers.